MEMPHIS TRAVEL GUIDE

2024 Edition

Hidden Gems and Local Secrets: Insider Tips for an Authentic Memphis Experience

Paul Patton

TABLE OF CONTENT

Important Notice Before You Continue Reading!

A unique travel experience awaits you within these pages. Step into a realm where extraordinary experiences lie within the pages of this exceptional travel guide. Our mission is simple: to ignite your imagination, fuel your creativity, and awaken the daring adventurer within you. Unlike conventional guides, we choose to forgo images, as we firmly believe in the power of firsthand discovery—unfiltered and uninfluenced by preconceptions. Prepare yourself for an enchanting voyage, where each monument, every corner, and every hidden gem eagerly await your personal encounter. Why spoil the exhilaration of that first glimpse, that overwhelming sense of awe? Get ready to embark on an unparalleled journey, where the vessel propelling you forward is none other than your boundless imagination, and you will be the architect of your own destiny. Abandon any preconceived notions and find yourself transported to an authentic Memphian experience, a realm teeming with extraordinary revelations. Brace yourself, for the magic of this expedition begins now, and remember, the most breathtaking images will be the ones painted by your own eyes.

In stark contrast to traditional guides, this book rejects the need for detailed maps. Why, you ask? Because we fervently believe that the greatest discoveries occur when you lose yourself, when you surrender to the ebb and flow of your surroundings, and embrace the thrill of the unknown path. No predetermined itineraries, no precise directions—our intention is to liberate you, allowing you to explore Memphis on your terms, without boundaries or limitations. Surrender to the currents and unveil hidden treasures that no map could ever reveal. Embrace audacity, follow your instincts, and prepare to be astounded. The magic of this expedition commences in your world without maps, where roads materialize with each step, and the most extraordinary adventures await within the unexplored folds of the unknown.

introduction

In the heart of the American South, there exists a city that embodies the very essence of soul and rhythm, a city where history reverberates through the streets, where music fills the air, and where culinary traditions are a testament to a rich, diverse heritage. Welcome to Memphis, a destination unlike any other in the United States. Inside this guide, we invite you to embark on an unforgettable journey through this vibrant and iconic city, a place that stands as a living testament to the roots of American culture, blending the past and the present in perfect harmony.

Memphis, often referred to as the "Home of the Blues" and the "Birthplace of Rock 'n' Roll," boasts a unique allure, drawing travelers from every corner of the globe. The city's rich history and cultural significance are woven into its very fabric, and visitors quickly find themselves immersed in an atmosphere that resonates with stories of legendary musicians, civil rights heroes, and mouthwatering culinary delights.

From the moment you set foot on Beale Street, you'll hear the unmistakable chords of the blues seeping through the historic district's vibrant atmosphere. You'll walk the same paths as Elvis Presley, the King of Rock 'n' Roll, did in his early days. As you explore the city, you'll uncover hidden gems and iconic landmarks that have played a pivotal role in shaping the nation's music and social history. Memphis is a living museum, and we are here to be your guide, illuminating the past while celebrating the present.

This travel guide is more than just a collection of information; it's a heartfelt invitation to experience Memphis in all its glory. We'll take you on a journey from the banks of the mighty Mississippi River to the influential museums, restaurants, and neighborhoods that make Memphis the dynamic, culturally rich destination it is today. You'll discover the stories of people who dared to dream and make history in the process, leaving an indelible mark on the city and the world. The city's struggles and triumphs are evident in every aspect of Memphis life, from its music and art to its culinary traditions and the enduring spirit of its residents.

Throughout this guide, we'll navigate you through the city's neighborhoods, offering insight into the distinct characteristics of each, from the lively energy of downtown to the historic significance of Midtown and the authenticity of neighborhoods like Cooper-Young and South Main. Memphis is a city that breathes life into every street, and each one tells a different story.

But Memphis is more than just a musical destination. Its culinary traditions are a feast for the senses, offering a journey of flavors and dishes you won't find anywhere else. Whether you're indulging in mouthwatering barbecue, savoring the taste of soul food, or exploring a burgeoning food scene, we'll guide you to the finest dining experiences the city has to offer.

As you read on, you'll find invaluable tips and recommendations on accommodations, transportation, and planning your trip to Memphis. We've included insights into the city's festivals and events, ensuring you make the most of your visit by participating in the celebrations that punctuate Memphis's calendar.

Memphis is a city of revelations, and as you turn the pages of this guide, you'll uncover countless opportunities for inspiration, enjoyment, and appreciation of the unique cultural tapestry that is Memphis. So, whether you're planning a short getaway, a music pilgrimage, or an exploration of history and culture, this guide promises to be your ultimate travel companion, enriching your journey and ensuring that your visit to this extraordinary city is an unforgettable, once-in-a-lifetime experience. Let's begin this adventure together, and allow Memphis to unveil its many wonders before you.

Get ready to explore, indulge, and immerse yourself in Memphis's charm as we unveil the magic of this remarkable city.

Why you should Visit

Memphis, Tennessee, is a city with a rich and diverse heritage that beckons travelers from all corners of the globe. Known for its contributions to music, its deep-rooted history, and its vibrant culture, Memphis offers an experience that is unlike any other. Whether you're a history enthusiast, a music lover, or simply looking for an unforgettable adventure, Memphis has something to offer everyone. we'll explore the compelling reasons why you should visit Memphis and immerse yourself in its unique charm.

Music: The Heart and Soul of Memphis
Memphis is widely regarded as the birthplace of blues music and the home of rock 'n' roll. Beale Street, often referred to as the "Home of the Blues," is a historic street that has been the breeding ground for some of the most iconic musicians in history, including B.B. King, Elvis Presley, and Johnny Cash. When you visit Memphis, you can't miss the opportunity to stroll down Beale Street, listen to live blues performances, and soak in the soulful atmosphere of this musical mecca. Additionally, Graceland, Elvis Presley's former mansion, is a must-visit destination for fans of the King of Rock 'n' Roll.

Civil Rights History: A Lesson in Equality
Memphis played a pivotal role in the American Civil Rights Movement, and you can experience this history firsthand by

visiting the National Civil Rights Museum, which is built around the Lorraine Motel, where Dr. Martin Luther King Jr. was assassinated in 1968. The museum offers a powerful and thought-provoking journey through the struggle for civil rights in the United States, making it a significant destination for anyone interested in social justice and equality.

Rich Culinary Traditions: A Taste of the South

Memphis is famous for its distinctive style of barbecue, and the city is home to some of the best barbecue joints in the country. Whether you prefer pulled pork, ribs, or chicken, Memphis has it all, and the local flavors are a testament to the city's culinary heritage. Sampling mouthwatering barbecue is a quintessential Memphis experience, but the city's culinary offerings extend beyond BBQ, with a thriving food scene that includes soul food, catfish, and more.

Unique Cultural Experiences

Memphis is a city that thrives on its unique cultural offerings. The city hosts various festivals and events throughout the year, celebrating its diverse heritage. Events like the Memphis in May International Festival, the Memphis Music and Heritage Festival, and the Memphis Film Festival showcase the city's rich culture, music, and arts. You can also explore vibrant neighborhoods like Cooper-Young, Overton Square, and South Main, which are filled with boutiques, galleries, and restaurants that reflect the city's creative spirit.

Soulful Art and Museums

Memphis is not only about music and history; it's also home to a thriving art scene. The Stax Museum of American Soul Music is a unique place to explore the history of soul music and its legendary artists. The Memphis Brooks Museum of Art features a diverse collection of artworks from different time periods and cultures. Whether you're interested in music, history, or art, Memphis offers a plethora of museums and cultural institutions to quench your thirst for knowledge and creativity.

Outdoor Adventures and Natural Beauty

For nature lovers, Memphis has a lot to offer. Shelby Farms Park, one of the largest urban parks in the United States, provides opportunities for hiking, biking, picnicking, and even horseback riding. The Mississippi River, which flows alongside Memphis, offers scenic riverboat cruises and the chance to appreciate the city's waterfront views. The city's green spaces and outdoor activities provide a refreshing contrast to its vibrant urban scene.

Memphis, Tennessee, is a city that invites you to immerse yourself in its soulful music, rich history, delicious cuisine, and vibrant culture. Whether you're wandering down Beale Street, exploring civil rights history, indulging in mouthwatering barbecue, or taking in the diverse cultural experiences, Memphis has something for everyone. It's a city that will leave an indelible mark on your heart and soul, making it a destination that you should not miss on your travel bucket list

Culture & Customs

This vibrant city on the banks of the Mississippi River has a unique blend of traditions, music, and cuisine that has captivated the hearts of locals and visitors alike for generations. Let's delve into the culture and customs that make Memphis such a fascinating place.

1. Music: The Heartbeat of Memphis

Memphis is synonymous with music. It's the city where the magic of blues, soul, and rock 'n' roll was born. Beale Street, a historic district in downtown Memphis, is often called the

"Home of the Blues" and remains a mecca for music lovers. This vibrant street is lined with clubs and bars where you can listen to live performances of these iconic genres any night of the week. Graceland, the former home of Elvis Presley, is another musical landmark that draws thousands of pilgrims each year.

The Memphis Sound has a unique history. It's where legends like B.B. King, Johnny Cash, and Otis Redding honed their craft. Sun Studio, also known as the "Birthplace of Rock 'n' Roll," is where Elvis Presley, Jerry Lee Lewis, and many other rock pioneers recorded their first tracks. Memphis' music culture is a blend of sorrowful blues, spirited soul, and energetic rock 'n' roll.

2. Southern Hospitality: A Memphis Tradition

Memphis is renowned for its warm and welcoming atmosphere. Southern hospitality is deeply ingrained in the city's culture, and visitors often remark on the friendliness of the locals. Whether you're at a local BBQ joint or exploring historical sites, you're likely to be greeted with a smile and a "How y'all doin'?"

Hospitality extends to the realm of food, too. Memphians take great pride in their culinary customs, and the city's barbecue is famous worldwide. Memphis-style BBQ is characterized by slow-cooked, smoked meats (often pork) slathered in a tangy, tomato-based sauce. The "pulled pork sandwich" is a local favorite, and you can find numerous BBQ joints around the city, each with its unique flavor and traditions.

3. History and Heritage: Preserving the Past

Memphis is a city that respects and preserves its history and heritage. The National Civil Rights Museum at the Lorraine Motel is one of the city's most significant cultural institutions. Located at the site of Dr. Martin Luther King Jr.'s assassination, the museum tells the story of the civil rights movement in the United States. It's a powerful reminder of the struggles and triumphs that have shaped the city's culture.

Beale Street, with its historic charm, takes you back in time to an era when the blues and jazz were king. The ornate theaters and historic landmarks of the city are testaments to its deep roots in American history and culture.

4. Festivals and Celebrations

Memphis knows how to celebrate, and the city hosts numerous festivals and events throughout the year. The Beale Street Music Festival, Memphis in May International Festival, and the Memphis Music and Heritage Festival are just a few of the annual events that showcase the city's musical talent, culinary delights, and cultural diversity. These festivals not only celebrate Memphis' heritage but also bring the community and tourists together in a harmonious blend of customs and traditions.

5. Art and Creativity: A Booming Scene

While music is undoubtedly the most famous aspect of Memphis' creative culture, the city also boasts a thriving arts and creative scene. The Memphis Brooks Museum of Art, the Dixon Gallery and Gardens, and the Metal Museum are just a few of the city's institutions that celebrate the visual arts. Street art and mural projects have also added a colorful, contemporary dimension to Memphis' cultural landscape.

6. Religious Diversity

Memphis is home to a variety of religious denominations, with a strong presence of Christian, Baptist, and Methodist communities. Many historic churches and synagogues dot the city's landscape, reflecting the diverse religious customs and traditions of its residents.

Memphis is a city where the past and present intermingle seamlessly. The deep-rooted music culture, soulful food, and rich history contribute to the unique customs that define this vibrant metropolis. The warmth and hospitality of its residents, along with their profound respect for their heritage, make Memphis a place unlike any other, offering visitors a chance to immerse themselves in a tapestry of customs that celebrate the very essence of American culture. Whether you're a music enthusiast, a foodie, a history buff, or an art lover, Memphis has something to offer, making it a city that leaves an indelible mark on anyone fortunate enough to experience its unique customs and culture.

Planning Your Trip

Best time to visit

To make the most of your trip to this iconic city, it's important to consider the best time to visit. We'll explore the different seasons and events that can help you plan your perfect Memphis getaway.

Spring: March to May

Spring in Memphis is a wonderful time to visit, as the city comes to life with blooming flowers, milder temperatures, and a variety of events. Here's what you can expect during the spring months:

Pleasant Weather: With temperatures ranging from 60°F to 75°F, spring provides ideal weather for outdoor activities and exploring Memphis's attractions comfortably.

Beale Street Music Festival: Held in early May, this three-day music festival features a diverse lineup of artists and takes place at Tom Lee Park, offering a fantastic kickstart to the festival season.

Memphis in May International Festival: This month-long celebration highlights Memphis's cultural diversity, with events like the World Championship Barbecue Cooking Contest, the Beale Street Music Festival, and the Sunset Symphony.

Fewer Crowds: Spring is a shoulder season, meaning fewer tourists compared to the summer months, making it a great time to enjoy popular sites without the hustle and bustle.

Summer: June to August

Memphis summers are hot and humid, but they offer plenty of exciting events and festivals. Keep these points in mind if you plan to visit during this time:

Graceland: Summer is the busiest season for Elvis fans as they flock to Graceland, Elvis Presley's former home, in droves.

Memphis Redbirds Baseball: Catch a game at AutoZone Park and enjoy America's favorite pastime during the summer months.

Memphis Botanic Garden: If you're a nature lover, this is the best time to explore the beautiful gardens and green spaces in and around the city.

Stay Hydrated: Make sure to stay hydrated and protect yourself from the heat if you visit during the peak of summer.

Fall: September to November
Autumn is another popular time to experience Memphis, with its moderate weather and a variety of festivals and events:

Memphis Zoo: Fall is a perfect time to visit the Memphis Zoo, as the animals are more active in the cooler weather.

Memphis International Jazz Festival: Celebrate the rich jazz history of the city in September with world-class performances.

Beautiful Fall Foliage: Enjoy the stunning fall foliage at Shelby Farms Park and other scenic areas in and around Memphis.

Lower Hotel Rates: Hotel rates often drop in the fall compared to the summer, making it a more budget-friendly time to visit.

Winter: December to February

While winters in Memphis are relatively mild compared to other parts of the United States, it's a quieter time to visit the city:

Graceland Holiday Lighting Ceremony: Experience the magic of Graceland during the holiday season when it's beautifully decorated and lit up.

Memphis Riverfront: Take a peaceful stroll along the Mississippi River and enjoy the scenic views without the summer crowds.

Memphis Grizzlies Basketball: Catch an NBA game and support the local team during the winter months.

Fewer Tourists: Winter is the least crowded time to explore Memphis, allowing you to enjoy its attractions at a leisurely pace.

The best time to visit Memphis largely depends on your preferences, but each season offers a unique experience. Whether you're drawn to the vibrant festivals of spring, the energy of summer, the colorful foliage of fall, or the tranquility of winter, Memphis has something to offer year-round. Plan your visit accordingly and make the most of this iconic Southern city's culture, history, and charm.

Visa and Travel Requirements

Whether you're coming for the blues, barbecue, or to explore the city's historical significance, it's essential to be well-prepared in terms of visa and travel requirements. This comprehensive guide will help you navigate the process of visiting Memphis, including essential visa information, travel tips, and other important considerations.

Visa Requirements
Visa Waiver Program (VWP)
The Visa Waiver Program (VWP) is a valuable option for citizens of certain countries wishing to visit the United States, including the vibrant city of Memphis, for short-term tourism or business purposes without the need for a traditional visa. As of my last knowledge update in September 2021, the VWP offered this privilege to numerous countries, including the United Kingdom, Germany, France, Australia, and several others. However, it's crucial to stay informed about any potential changes to VWP eligibility by referring to the official website of the U.S. Department of State.

Who is Eligible for VWP?
Citizens of VWP countries enjoy the following privileges when traveling to the United States:

Visa-Free Entry: Travelers from VWP countries can enter the United States for up to 90 days without obtaining a B-2 tourist visa, as long as their visit is for tourism, business, or family visits.

Business Activities: VWP visitors can participate in activities related to their business, such as attending meetings, conferences, and negotiating contracts. However, they cannot engage in gainful employment during their stay.

Tourism: Memphis, with its rich cultural heritage, is a popular destination for tourists. VWP travelers can explore the city's iconic landmarks, music heritage, and vibrant culture during their 90-day stay.

Electronic System for Travel Authorization (ESTA)
While the VWP offers flexibility, it is vital to note that travelers entering the United States under the VWP are

required to obtain an approved Electronic System for Travel Authorization (ESTA) before boarding their flight. ESTA is an online system designed to pre-screen travelers and determine their eligibility to enter the U.S. under the VWP.

Here are the key points regarding ESTA:

Online Application: Travelers must complete the ESTA application online, providing personal information, travel details, and passport information. It's recommended to apply for ESTA well in advance of your travel date, ideally at least 72 hours before your departure. However, it's advisable to apply even earlier to ensure timely processing.

Payment: There is a nominal fee associated with the ESTA application. Payment can be made online using a credit card.

Approval and Authorization: Typically, ESTA approval is granted quickly, often within minutes. Once approved, the authorization is valid for two years or until your passport expires, whichever comes first. This means that if you have a valid ESTA, you can make multiple trips to the United States under the VWP within that two-year period.

Keep a Record: It's essential to keep a record of your ESTA approval. Although it's electronically linked to your passport, it's wise to have a printed or digital copy as a backup.

Non-VWP Countries

If your country is not part of the Visa Waiver Program, you will need to apply for a U.S. tourist visa, specifically a B-2 visa, through the U.S. Embassy or Consulate in your home country. Here's what you should know:

Application Process: Applying for a B-2 tourist visa involves a detailed process. It typically includes completing an application form, providing necessary documentation, attending an interview at the U.S. Embassy or Consulate, and paying a visa fee.

Varied Requirements: Visa application requirements, such as the documentation needed and the specific procedures, may vary depending on the U.S. Embassy or Consulate in your home country. Therefore, it's crucial to check the specific requirements and processing times for your location.

Advance Planning: Given the potential variation in visa processing times and the need for an interview, it is highly advisable to initiate the application process well in advance of your intended trip to Memphis. This ensures that you have sufficient time to complete all the necessary steps and obtain your visa before your travel date.

Travel Preparations
Passport
Before making travel plans, ensure that your passport is valid for at least six months beyond your intended departure from the United States. It's also advisable to make a photocopy of your passport and store it separately from the original in case of loss or theft.

Travel Insurance
While not mandatory, having travel insurance is highly recommended. Travel insurance can provide coverage for medical emergencies, trip cancellations, and other unforeseen events that may disrupt your travel plans.

Flight Reservations
Book your flights to Memphis well in advance to secure the best deals and ensure availability. Memphis International

Airport (MEM) is the primary airport serving the city, with numerous domestic and some international flights.

Important Contact Information
Make a list of essential contact information, including the local U.S. Embassy or Consulate, emergency numbers (911 for emergencies), and your country's embassy or consulate in the United States.

Visiting Memphis is an exciting experience filled with history, music, and delicious cuisine. By ensuring you've met all the necessary visa and travel requirements, you can focus on enjoying the city's vibrant atmosphere and everything it has to offer. Remember that travel regulations and requirements can change, so always check with official sources for the most up-to-date information before your trip.

What to pack
Whether you're planning to explore its iconic music scene, indulge in mouthwatering barbecue, or immerse yourself in its rich heritage, it's important to pack wisely to ensure a comfortable and enjoyable trip. Here's a guide on what to pack when visiting Memphis.

1. Weather-Appropriate Clothing:
Memphis experiences a range of weather conditions throughout the year. Summers are hot and humid, while winters can be cold and damp. Spring and fall offer milder temperatures. Pack accordingly:

In summer (June to August), bring lightweight clothing, sunglasses, and sunscreen to beat the heat.
Winters (December to February) require warm layers, a jacket, and an umbrella for occasional rain.
2. Comfortable Footwear:

With so much to see and do in Memphis, comfortable walking shoes are a must. You'll be exploring Beale Street, Graceland, and many other attractions, so prioritize comfort over style.

3. Insect Repellent:
Mosquitoes can be a nuisance, especially in the warmer months. To avoid itchy bites, pack insect repellent to use when exploring outdoor attractions like the Mississippi River Park or Shelby Farms Park.

4. Electrical Adapters:
If you're traveling from outside the United States, ensure you bring the necessary electrical adapters or converters for your devices, as Memphis uses the standard American two-pin plug.

5. Travel Guide and Maps:
Even in the age of smartphones, having a physical travel guide and maps can be invaluable for navigating Memphis's streets, especially if you're in areas with poor mobile network coverage.

6. Musical Necessities:
Memphis is synonymous with music, so don't forget to pack:

Earplugs for live music venues, as it can get loud.
A portable speaker to enjoy some tunes along the Mississippi River.
Your favorite music streaming app downloaded for easy access to the city's legendary songs.

7. Cash and Credit Cards:
While most places accept credit cards, it's a good idea to carry some cash, especially for small vendors and markets. ATMs are widely available in the city.

8. Reusable Water Bottle:
The Memphis sun can be scorching, so stay hydrated by bringing a reusable water bottle. You can fill it up at public water fountains or ask for refills in cafes and restaurants.

9. Travel Insurance:
It's always wise to have travel insurance to cover any unexpected mishaps, including medical emergencies or trip cancellations.

10. A Good Appetite:
Memphis is renowned for its mouthwatering barbecue and soul food. Come with an empty stomach and a sense of culinary adventure. Don't forget to pack your appetite and be ready to indulge in the city's delectable offerings.

11. Camera and Chargers:
Capture the vibrant culture and history of Memphis by bringing your camera, along with its charger and extra memory cards. The city's sights and sounds are perfect for creating lasting memories.

12. Respectful Attire:
Remember that Memphis has a rich cultural and historical heritage. When visiting places like the National Civil Rights Museum, dress respectfully and be mindful of local customs and traditions.

13. Sun Protection:
Sunscreen, a wide-brimmed hat, and sunglasses are essential for the sunny Memphis days. The sun can be strong, and protecting your skin and eyes is important.

14. Entertainment for Downtime:
Whether you're waiting at the airport or relaxing in your hotel room, bring books, magazines, or entertainment options to pass the time during downtime.

Memphis offers a unique blend of history, music, and delicious cuisine, making it a must-visit destination for travelers. By packing wisely and considering the specific needs of the city, you'll be well-prepared for an unforgettable experience in this vibrant and culturally rich southern gem. Enjoy your trip to Memphis!

Trip Planning Tools

Whether you're a music enthusiast hoping to explore the birthplace of rock 'n' roll or a foodie looking to savor some mouthwatering barbecue, a well-planned trip to Memphis is essential. To help you make the most of your visit, we'll discuss some essential trip planning tools to ensure your time in Memphis is memorable and stress-free.

Online Travel Guides: Start your trip planning by browsing through online travel guides dedicated to Memphis. Websites like TripAdvisor, Lonely Planet, and even official city websites offer valuable insights into the city's attractions, events, and accommodations. These guides often include tips on the best time to visit, must-see destinations, and local cultural norms.

Memphis Visitors Bureau: The Memphis Convention & Visitors Bureau (CVB) is a fantastic resource for trip planning. Their website provides comprehensive information on accommodations, dining, events, and attractions. Additionally, you can visit their physical office in downtown Memphis for personalized recommendations, brochures, and maps.

Mobile Apps: Download travel apps like TripAdvisor, Yelp, or Google Maps to help you navigate Memphis with ease. These apps offer user reviews, real-time traffic updates, and suggestions for local restaurants and attractions. Memphis also has its own app, "Memphis Travel," which includes itineraries, event listings, and a variety of discounts for visitors.

Accommodation Booking Websites: Platforms like Booking.com, Airbnb, and Expedia are excellent resources for finding the best accommodation options in Memphis. Depending on your budget and preferences, you can choose from a wide range of hotels, vacation rentals, and B&Bs.

Event Calendars: Memphis is renowned for its vibrant music scene, with Beale Street hosting live performances almost every night. To plan your visit around specific events, check online event calendars like MemphisTravel.com or local newspapers. You might find jazz festivals, blues performances, or cultural festivals happening during your stay.

Transportation Tools: Memphis is well-connected with a major airport, Amtrak train service, and an extensive bus network. Use flight booking websites like Kayak, Expedia, or Google Flights to find the best airfare deals. For local transportation, consider the Memphis Area Transit Authority (MATA) website or mobile apps for bus routes and schedules.

CityPASS: If you're looking to visit multiple attractions, consider purchasing a Memphis CityPASS. This pass offers discounted admission to top destinations such as Graceland, the National Civil Rights Museum, and the Memphis Zoo. It's a cost-effective way to explore the city's most iconic sites.

Weather Forecast: Memphis experiences a wide range of weather conditions throughout the year. Check a reliable weather forecasting website or app to ensure your packing is appropriate for the season. Be prepared for hot and humid summers and occasionally chilly winters.

Local Blogs and Forums: Don't underestimate the value of local insight. Blogs and forums dedicated to Memphis can provide you with real experiences and tips from residents and frequent visitors. They might suggest hidden gems that you won't find in mainstream travel guides.

Travel Insurance: While planning your trip, consider purchasing travel insurance. This can protect you in case of unexpected cancellations, delays, or health emergencies. Be sure to read the policy carefully to understand what is covered.

Restaurant Reservations: Memphis is renowned for its delectable cuisine, especially its barbecue. If you plan to dine at popular restaurants, make reservations in advance. Tools like OpenTable or calling the restaurant directly can help secure your table.

Local Maps: While GPS is convenient, having a physical map of Memphis can be invaluable. You can obtain maps at the Visitors Bureau or print them out from online sources. These maps often include the locations of major attractions, streets, and neighborhoods.

Memphis is a city brimming with culture, history, and entertainment. Effective trip planning tools are essential to ensure a smooth and enjoyable visit. By using online resources, mobile apps, and local insights, you can make the most of your trip to Memphis, experiencing its legendary music, mouthwatering food, and the warmth of Southern hospitality. So, take your time, plan well, and get ready to immerse yourself in the heart and soul of this incredible city.

How to avoid tourist trap?

Like any popular tourist destination, Memphis has its fair share of tourist traps. These are places and activities that are often overpriced, crowded, and may not provide an authentic experience. To truly enjoy your visit and experience the real Memphis, it's essential to know how to avoid these tourist traps.

Be Cautious on Beale Street:

Beale Street is iconic in Memphis, known for its live music, clubs, and nightlife. While it's a must-visit for many tourists, it can also be a tourist trap. To avoid disappointment, go during off-peak hours or weekdays when it's less crowded. Many establishments on Beale Street have cover charges or overpriced drinks during peak times. To save money, do your research and find venues that offer happy hour specials or live music without a cover charge.

Skip Chain Restaurants:

Memphis is famous for its barbecue, soul food, and other local cuisine. While it might be tempting to dine at well-known chain restaurants, it's best to seek out local, family-owned establishments. Chain restaurants tend to offer generic, mass-produced versions of Memphis classics, which won't give you an authentic taste of the city.

Explore Beyond Graceland:

Graceland is a major tourist attraction in Memphis, the former home of Elvis Presley. While it's a significant part of Memphis history, it can be quite crowded and expensive. If you're an Elvis fan, by all means, visit Graceland, but remember that there's much more to Memphis than the King of Rock 'n' Roll. Explore other attractions like the Stax Museum of American Soul Music, Sun Studio, and the National Civil Rights Museum for a more well-rounded experience.

Visit the Real Beale Street Historic District:
While Beale Street is famous, many tourists mistakenly visit the wrong portion of it. The actual Beale Street Historic District is only a few blocks long and is where you'll find the most authentic Memphis music scene. Avoid wandering too far from this district, as the further you go, the more likely you are to stumble upon tourist traps.

Avoid Street Touts:
You'll find street touts or hawkers on Beale Street and in other popular tourist areas. They'll often offer tickets to attractions, tours, or overpriced merchandise. Avoid making impulsive decisions based on their recommendations, and instead, do your research before buying tickets or signing up for tours. There are many reputable tour operators and ticket sellers in Memphis, so it's better to seek them out in advance.

Plan Your Visit During Off-Peak Seasons:
Memphis experiences peak tourist seasons during holidays and major events, such as the Beale Street Music Festival and Memphis in May. Prices tend to be higher, and crowds can be overwhelming during these times. To avoid tourist traps, consider planning your visit during the off-peak seasons, like late fall or early spring when the weather is pleasant, and the city is less crowded.

Explore Beyond Downtown:
While downtown Memphis has much to offer, don't limit your exploration to this area alone. Venture out to other neighborhoods like Midtown, Cooper-Young, and South Main. These areas have their own unique charm, local businesses, and cultural attractions. You'll find a more authentic Memphis experience when you explore these neighborhoods.

Read Reviews and Do Research:

Before visiting any attraction or restaurant, read reviews on platforms like TripAdvisor, Yelp, and Google. Travel forums and blogs are also excellent resources for gathering information about what to expect. By doing your research, you can identify potential tourist traps and choose more authentic options.

Attend Local Events:
One of the best ways to immerse yourself in the local culture and avoid tourist traps is to attend local events. Memphis hosts various festivals, concerts, and cultural events throughout the year. These events provide a chance to interact with locals and experience the city's vibrant culture.

Stay in a Local Neighborhood:
When choosing accommodation, consider staying in a local neighborhood rather than a chain hotel in the heart of downtown. This allows you to experience the city like a local, with easy access to neighborhood eateries and shops. It can also be more budget-friendly and less tourist-oriented.

Seek Out Hidden Gems:
Memphis is full of hidden gems that often go unnoticed by tourists. Talk to locals, ask for recommendations, and explore lesser-known spots. Whether it's a hidden park, a neighborhood bakery, or a historic site, these hidden gems can provide a more authentic and less touristy experience.

Memphis has a lot to offer beyond its tourist traps. By being a savvy traveler, doing your research, and seeking out local experiences, you can enjoy the true essence of this vibrant city. From exploring its rich music history to savoring its delicious cuisine, there's much to discover in Memphis that doesn't involve falling into the typical tourist traps. So, get out there and experience the Memphis that the locals know and love.

Accommodation

Best Neighborhood to stay

Memphis offers a variety of neighborhoods, each with its own unique character and attractions. we'll explore some of the best neighborhoods to stay when visiting Memphis, so you can make the most of your trip to this vibrant city.

Downtown Memphis

Downtown Memphis is the heart of the city, and it's a great choice for visitors who want to be at the center of the action. Beale Street, famous for its live music, clubs, and vibrant atmosphere, is a highlight of downtown. The National Civil Rights Museum, located at the former Lorraine Motel where Martin Luther King Jr. was assassinated, is another major attraction. Staying in downtown Memphis means you'll be close to these historic sites, as well as the Mississippi River, where you can take a riverboat cruise.

Downtown also features several upscale hotels, making it a popular choice for those who want a more luxurious stay. You'll find excellent dining options and a lively nightlife scene. Additionally, the trolley system in downtown makes it easy to explore other parts of the city.

Midtown Memphis

Midtown Memphis is known for its artistic and bohemian vibe. This neighborhood is home to the Memphis Zoo, the Memphis Brooks Museum of Art, and the Memphis College of Art. The historic Cooper-Young district is a hub for local shops, restaurants, and live music. If you want a more laid-back and artsy experience during your visit, Midtown is an excellent choice.

Cooper-Young offers a wide range of accommodation options, from charming bed and breakfasts to boutique hotels. It's also a great area to explore on foot, with tree-lined streets and unique boutiques. Additionally, Overton Park, located in Midtown, is a beautiful urban green space where you can relax and enjoy outdoor activities.

East Memphis

East Memphis is a more residential and business-oriented area. This is a suitable choice for those who prefer a quieter atmosphere and easy access to shopping and dining. The neighborhood features shopping centers like Oak Court Mall and a variety of upscale restaurants.

One of the key attractions in East Memphis is Shelby Farms Park, one of the largest urban parks in the United States. It offers numerous outdoor activities, including biking, hiking, horseback riding, and paddle boating. If you're traveling with family, you might consider staying in East Memphis for its family-friendly environment and spacious accommodations.

South Main Arts District

South Main Arts District is a trendy and up-and-coming area in Memphis. It's known for its art galleries, boutique shops, and a thriving arts scene. Staying here will put you in close proximity to the Memphis Farmers Market, which operates on Saturdays, and the historic Arcade Restaurant, the oldest café in Memphis.

The area is particularly popular among young and creative individuals, and you can find unique loft-style accommodations and hip boutique hotels. It's also close to iconic landmarks like the National Civil Rights Museum, making it a convenient base for history enthusiasts.

Cooper-Young Historic District

Cooper-Young is a lively and eclectic neighborhood that's a fantastic choice for those seeking a diverse range of dining and entertainment options. It's home to countless restaurants, bars, and shops, making it a hub for foodies and those who appreciate local culture. The district is known for its historic bungalows and a welcoming, laid-back atmosphere.

Cooper-Young offers a mix of accommodation options, including charming bed and breakfasts and vacation rentals. It's a neighborhood where you can experience the charm of Memphis and explore its vibrant local culture.

Harbor Town

For a unique experience, consider staying in Harbor Town, a picturesque neighborhood located on Mud Island. It's a quieter area with beautiful river views and upscale dining options. Mud Island River Park, known for its Riverwalk and amphitheater, is a key attraction in this neighborhood.

Harbor Town is a bit removed from the hustle and bustle of downtown but offers a serene and scenic setting for a more relaxed visit. It's a great choice for couples looking for a romantic getaway.

Germantown

Germantown is a lovely suburb of Memphis known for its upscale atmosphere and beautiful residential areas. It's a bit farther from the city center, making it an excellent choice for those who want a peaceful and serene environment. Germantown offers high-end shopping and dining experiences, as well as access to the Shelby Farms Greenline, a scenic urban trail perfect for biking and walking.

When staying in Germantown, you can enjoy the tranquility of suburban life while still being within a reasonable driving distance of downtown Memphis and its attractions.

Each neighborhood has its unique appeal, so your choice will depend on your preferences and interests. Whether you want to be in the heart of the action in downtown, experience the artsy atmosphere of Midtown, or enjoy the tranquility of a suburb like Germantown, Memphis has something to offer every type of traveler. The neighborhood you choose can significantly impact your overall Memphis experience, so take your time to explore your options and find the one that suits you best

Top luxury Hotel

Memphis is a city known for its rich history, music, and vibrant culture, and there are numerous options for luxury hotels that offer both comfort and convenience. we will explore some luxury hotels in Memphis, complete with their addresses, to help you make an informed choice for your stay.

The Peabody Memphis

Address: 149 Union Ave, Memphis, TN 38103
Description: The Peabody Memphis is an iconic hotel that has been a staple of Memphis hospitality for over 150 years. Its grand lobby, world-famous ducks that march daily, and elegant rooms make it a prime choice for luxury travelers. With its central location, it's easy to explore Beale Street, the National Civil Rights Museum, and other Memphis attractions.

The Guest House at Graceland

Address: 3600 Elvis Presley Blvd, Memphis, TN 38116
Description: For fans of Elvis Presley, there's no better place to stay than The Guest House at Graceland. Located just steps away from Graceland Mansion, this luxurious hotel offers Elvis-inspired suites and a warm, Southern hospitality. It's a tribute to the King of Rock 'n' Roll's legacy and offers a unique experience for his admirers.

Hu. Hotel

Address: 79 Madison Ave, Memphis, TN 38103
Description: Hu. Hotel is a chic, modern boutique hotel located in downtown Memphis. It boasts stylish and contemporary rooms, a rooftop bar with stunning city views, and an exceptional on-site restaurant. This hotel provides an urban oasis for travelers who appreciate a blend of luxury and artistic flair.

The River Inn of Harbor Town

Address: 50 Harbor Town Square, Memphis, TN 38103
Description: If you seek a peaceful, riverside escape in Memphis, The River Inn of Harbor Town is an excellent choice. Nestled along the Mississippi River, this luxury boutique hotel offers scenic views, upscale dining at Paulette's, and elegantly appointed rooms. It's a serene retreat from the city's hustle and bustle.

Big Cypress Lodge

Address: 1 Bass Pro Dr, Memphis, TN 38105
Description: For a truly unique lodging experience, consider staying at Big Cypress Lodge. Located inside the massive Bass Pro Shops at the Pyramid, this hotel features rustic yet luxurious accommodations, including rooms with stunning views of an indoor swamp, complete with alligators. It's an adventure within a hotel, perfect for nature enthusiasts.

The Westin Memphis Beale Street

Address: 170 Lt George W Lee Ave, Memphis, TN 38103
Description: Situated right on Beale Street, The Westin Memphis Beale Street offers convenience and luxury in one. Guests can enjoy spacious rooms, a rooftop pool, and direct

access to Beale Street's vibrant music scene. It's an ideal choice for those who want to immerse themselves in the heart of Memphis.

Madison Hotel

Address: 79 Madison Ave, Memphis, TN 38103
Description: Madison Hotel is a sophisticated and artfully designed boutique hotel in downtown Memphis. With its timeless charm, luxurious accommodations, and a rooftop lounge providing panoramic city views, it's a perfect choice for travelers seeking an intimate and elegant stay.

The Central Station Memphis

Address: 545 S Main St, Memphis, TN 38103
Description: Housed in a historic train station, The Central Station Memphis offers a unique blend of nostalgia and contemporary luxury. This boutique hotel features stylish rooms, an award-winning restaurant, and easy access to the South Main Arts District. It's an excellent option for those who appreciate history and culture.

Whether you prefer the classic elegance of The Peabody, the rock 'n' roll legacy of The Guest House at Graceland, or the modern sophistication of Hu. Hotel, you're sure to find the perfect accommodation to make your Memphis visit a memorable one. Remember to book your stay in advance, as these luxury hotels tend to be in high demand, especially during peak travel seasons. Enjoy your stay in the birthplace of the blues and the home of

Budget friendly Hotels to Stay in

1. Comfort Inn Downtown Memphis

Address: 100 N Front St, Memphis, TN 38103
Description: Comfort Inn Downtown Memphis is an excellent choice for travelers seeking comfort and affordability. Located in the heart of downtown Memphis, this hotel provides easy access to many popular attractions, including Beale Street, Graceland, and the National Civil Rights Museum. The rooms are well-appointed, and the hotel offers complimentary breakfast and Wi-Fi. The friendly staff ensures a pleasant stay, and the convenient location makes it a top pick for budget-conscious travelers.

2. Super 8 by Wyndham Memphis/Downtown/Graceland Area

Address: 1111 E Brooks Rd, Memphis, TN 38116
Description: Super 8 by Wyndham Memphis/Downtown/Graceland Area offers a great value for your stay in Memphis. Situated close to Graceland and the Memphis International Airport, it's a convenient choice for those interested in Elvis Presley's legacy. The hotel features clean and comfortable rooms with essential amenities, and guests can enjoy a complimentary breakfast. The friendly staff and easy access to attractions make this a wallet-friendly option.

3. La Quinta Inn & Suites by Wyndham Memphis Downtown

Address: 310 Union Ave, Memphis, TN 38103
Description: Located in the heart of downtown Memphis, La Quinta Inn & Suites offers a comfortable stay without breaking the bank. The hotel is within walking distance of Beale Street, the Orpheum Theatre, and the Mississippi

Riverfront. Guests can enjoy spacious rooms, a complimentary breakfast, and a fitness center. The staff is known for their friendly service, and the central location ensures you can explore the city without hassle.

4. Days Inn by Wyndham Memphis at Graceland

Address: 3839 Elvis Presley Blvd, Memphis, TN 38116
Description: If your visit to Memphis revolves around Graceland, Days Inn by Wyndham Memphis at Graceland is an excellent choice. This budget-friendly hotel is just a short walk from Elvis Presley's famous mansion. The hotel offers clean and comfortable rooms with modern amenities, and guests can take advantage of a complimentary continental breakfast. The proximity to Graceland makes it an ideal option for Elvis fans on a budget.

5. Motel 6 Memphis, TN - Graceland

Address: 1581 E Brooks Rd, Memphis, TN 38116
Description: For travelers looking for a no-frills, budget-friendly stay near Graceland, Motel 6 Memphis is a suitable option. The rooms are simple but clean, and the hotel offers great value for the price. Being close to Graceland, it's a convenient choice for Elvis enthusiasts. Plus, it's just a short drive from the Memphis International Airport, making it accessible for those arriving by air.

6. Quality Inn Memphis Airport

Address: 1587 E Brooks Rd, Memphis, TN 38116
Description: Quality Inn Memphis Airport is another affordable option located near Graceland and Memphis International Airport. The hotel provides comfortable accommodations, including a complimentary breakfast and Wi-Fi. The friendly staff is always ready to assist, making

your stay enjoyable. Its proximity to both Graceland and the airport makes it a practical choice for budget-conscious travelers.

7. Red Roof Inn Memphis - Airport

Address: 3265 Elvis Presley Blvd, Memphis, TN 38116
Description: Red Roof Inn Memphis - Airport is a wallet-friendly choice located near the airport and Graceland. The hotel offers clean and well-maintained rooms, and guests can enjoy free parking and Wi-Fi. This pet-friendly hotel provides a great value for travelers who want to explore both Elvis-related sites and the rest of Memphis.

8. Best Western Plus Gen X Inn

Address: 1177 Madison Ave, Memphis, TN 38104
Description: Best Western Plus Gen X Inn offers budget-conscious travelers a comfortable stay in the Midtown area of Memphis. The hotel is located near Overton Park, the Memphis Zoo, and the historic Sun Studio. Guests can enjoy spacious rooms with modern amenities, a complimentary hot breakfast, and a fitness center. This is an excellent choice for those looking to explore a more eclectic side of Memphis without compromising on quality.

9. Americas Best Value Inn & Suites Memphis

Address: 1360 Springbrook Ave, Memphis, TN 38116
Description: Americas Best Value Inn & Suites Memphis is a budget-friendly option close to Graceland and the Memphis International Airport. The hotel offers clean and cozy rooms, complimentary breakfast, and Wi-Fi. With its affordability and convenient location, it's a great choice for travelers interested in exploring the Elvis Presley legacy.

10. Rodeway Inn Memphis

Address: 1581 E Brooks Rd, Memphis, TN 38116
Description: Rodeway Inn Memphis offers budget-friendly accommodations near Graceland. The hotel provides simple yet comfortable rooms and a complimentary continental breakfast. It's an ideal choice for travelers who want to focus their visit on Elvis-related attractions while staying within their budget.

These budget-friendly hotel options in Memphis provide a range of choices for travelers seeking affordable accommodations while enjoying the city's rich musical and cultural heritage. Whether you're visiting Graceland, exploring downtown Memphis, or enjoying the city's many attractions, these hotels ensure you have a comfortable and budget-conscious stay.

Hostel & Guesthouse

To make the most of your visit, it's essential to choose accommodation that fits your budget and preferences. Hostels and guesthouses can be excellent choices for travelers seeking a more budget-friendly and communal experience. we'll explore some of the best hostels and guesthouses in Memphis, providing their addresses to help you make an informed choice.

Downtown Memphis Hostel

Address: 62 South Main Street, Memphis, TN 38103
Description: Located right in the heart of downtown Memphis, this hostel is the ideal place for budget-conscious travelers who want to be in the center of the action. The hostel offers both dormitory-style and private rooms, and it's within walking distance of iconic attractions such as Beale Street, the National Civil Rights Museum, and Graceland.

You'll also find a communal kitchen, free Wi-Fi, and a friendly atmosphere that makes it easy to meet fellow travelers.

Memphis Travelers Hostel

Address: 253 North B.B. King Boulevard, Memphis, TN 38103
Description: Memphis Travelers Hostel is another great option for those looking for affordable accommodation in the heart of the city. The hostel is known for its friendly staff, cozy common areas, and a variety of room options to suit different traveler preferences. Its proximity to the Mississippi River, Sun Studio, and St. Jude Children's Research Hospital makes it an excellent choice for those looking to explore Memphis's various attractions.

The Exchange Guesthouse

Address: 347 North Third Street, Memphis, TN 38105
Description: If you're seeking a more intimate and homey atmosphere, The Exchange Guesthouse is a charming boutique guesthouse with a limited number of rooms. Each room is uniquely decorated, and the guesthouse exudes a warm and inviting ambiance. It's close to Bass Pro Shops at the Pyramid, Mud Island River Park, and the Mississippi River, offering guests a peaceful escape in the city.

Vance Loft Guest House

Address: 198 Vance Avenue, Memphis, TN 38103
Description: For a more private and upscale guesthouse experience, Vance Loft Guest House is an excellent choice. Located in the historic South Main Arts District, this guesthouse offers luxurious and spacious suites, making it a perfect option for couples or travelers seeking a bit of

pampering. It's within walking distance of iconic landmarks like the Orpheum Theatre and the Mississippi River.

The Memphis International Hostel

Address: 316 Washington Avenue, Memphis, TN 38103
Description: The Memphis International Hostel offers a unique blend of affordability and convenience. It's situated in a historic building and is known for its friendly staff and diverse international crowd of guests. This hostel is within easy reach of attractions like the Memphis Zoo, Overton Park, and the Memphis Brooks Museum of Art.

Soulsville Hostel

Address: 1087 College Street, Memphis, TN 38106
Description: Located in the historic Soulsville USA neighborhood, this hostel is perfect for travelers interested in the rich musical heritage of Memphis. It's within walking distance of the Stax Museum of American Soul Music, the Memphis Rock 'n' Soul Museum, and the National Ornamental Metal Museum. The Soulsville Hostel offers a cozy and welcoming environment for guests.

Backbeat Hostel

Address: 61 Keel Avenue, Memphis, TN 38105
Description: Backbeat Hostel is a trendy and contemporary option for budget-conscious travelers. This hostel features a stylish design and comfortable accommodations, including dormitory-style rooms and private suites. It's close to attractions like the Mississippi River Park, the Mississippi River Museum, and the Mississippi Greenbelt Park, making it a great choice for outdoor enthusiasts.

Memphis is a city filled with history, music, and mouthwatering food, and your choice of accommodation can greatly enhance your overall travel experience. Whether you prefer the vibrant atmosphere of a downtown hostel or the intimate charm of a guesthouse, Memphis has a range of options to suit your needs and budget.

When selecting your hostel or guesthouse, consider factors such as location, amenities, and the type of experience you want. Each of these accommodation options provides a unique taste of Memphis, ensuring your visit to this iconic city is as memorable as the music that fills its streets. Whether you're a music enthusiast, a history buff, or a foodie, Memphis has something for everyone, and your choice of accommodation can make your trip all the more special. Enjoy your stay in Memphis and immerse yourself in the soulful rhythms of this remarkable city.

Top Tourist Attractions & Spots

Memphis, Tennessee offers a rich tapestry of attractions and experiences for visitors. Whether you're a music enthusiast, history buff, or simply seeking a memorable vacation, Memphis has something for everyone. Here, we'll explore some of the top tourist attractions and spots you should not miss when visiting Memphis, complete with their address;

1. Graceland

Address: 3734 Elvis Presley Blvd, Memphis, TN 38116
Graceland is the iconic former home of Elvis Presley, a cultural icon and the "King of Rock 'n' Roll." Visiting Graceland is like stepping into the private world of one of the most influential musicians in history. The mansion tour takes you through the rooms where Elvis lived, showcasing his exquisite taste in decor and design. You'll see the famous Jungle Room, the music room, and his racquetball building, now housing a museum filled with Elvis memorabilia.

Graceland's Meditation Garden is a serene and reflective space where Elvis and other family members are buried. Fans often leave tributes here. The Elvis Presley Car Museum displays a collection of the King's favorite automobiles, including his beloved Pink Cadillac.

The experience of Graceland is truly immersive and gives you a glimpse into the life and legacy of Elvis Presley. It's a must-visit for music enthusiasts and anyone interested in the history of rock 'n' roll.

2. Beale Street

Address: Beale St, Memphis, TN 38103
Beale Street is the historic heart of Memphis' entertainment district. This vibrant street, lined with neon lights, is a hub for live music, mouthwatering Southern cuisine, and a lively atmosphere. As you stroll down Beale Street, you'll hear the soulful sounds of blues, jazz, and rock 'n' roll emanating from the many clubs and bars.

Some famous establishments on Beale Street include B.B. King's Blues Club and Rum Boogie Cafe. You can enjoy everything from classic blues to modern rock here. If you're a music enthusiast, be sure to explore Beale Street at night when the music scene truly comes alive.

The street is also dotted with great restaurants offering Southern delicacies like barbecue, fried chicken, and catfish. It's an ideal place to savor Memphis' unique food culture. You can also find unique shops and boutiques selling everything from music memorabilia to eclectic souvenirs.

Beale Street is not just a tourist attraction; it's a cultural experience that showcases Memphis' rich musical heritage.

3. Sun Studio

Address: 706 Union Ave, Memphis, TN 38103
Sun Studio is often referred to as the "Birthplace of Rock 'n' Roll" because of its pivotal role in shaping the music industry. This modest studio is where legendary musicians like Elvis Presley, Johnny Cash, Jerry Lee Lewis, and B.B. King recorded some of their earliest hits.

A guided tour of Sun Studio offers visitors a chance to step back in time. You'll see the original recording equipment, vintage microphones, and even the X on the floor where Elvis stood when he recorded his first track. The tour guides share fascinating stories about the studio's history and the artists who made it famous.

The vibe at Sun Studio is electrifying, and it's easy to imagine the groundbreaking music that was created within these walls. For music lovers, this is a pilgrimage site that allows you to connect with the roots of rock 'n' roll.

4. Stax Museum of American Soul Music

Address: 926 E McLemore Ave, Memphis, TN 38126
The Stax Museum pays homage to the unique and soulful sound of American soul music. It's located at the original site of Stax Records, one of the most influential record labels in the history of soul music. The museum showcases the artists who recorded at Stax, including Otis Redding, Isaac Hayes, and Booker T. & the MGs.

As you step inside, you're greeted by the iconic image of the Stax sign that once graced the studio's façade. The museum is filled with memorabilia, including stage outfits, instruments, and even a replica of the studio control room. You can listen to classic tracks and watch videos that delve into the history of Stax Records.

The Stax Museum offers an in-depth look into the cultural and social impact of soul music and its contribution to the civil rights movement. It's a place where you can feel the soulful groove and understand the artists' struggle for equality.

5. National Civil Rights Museum

Address: 450 Mulberry St, Memphis, TN 38103

Housed in the former Lorraine Motel, the National Civil Rights Museum is a moving and powerful tribute to the civil rights movement in the United States. The museum tells the story of the struggle for racial equality, from the days of slavery through the Civil Rights era and into the present.

The most iconic exhibit is Room 306, where Dr. Martin Luther King Jr. was assassinated in 1968. This room, preserved as it was on that fateful day, is a poignant reminder of the sacrifices made for civil rights.

The museum's exhibits are extensive and thought-provoking, addressing issues such as segregation, the Montgomery Bus Boycott, and the March on Washington. It provides a comprehensive understanding of the long and challenging journey towards civil rights.

The National Civil Rights Museum is not just a historical site; it's a place of reflection, education, and inspiration. It's an essential visit for anyone interested in the ongoing struggle for equality and justice in America.

6. Memphis Zoo

Address: 2000 Prentiss Pl, Memphis, TN 38112
The Memphis Zoo is a fantastic family-friendly attraction, home to over 3,500 animals representing more than 500 species. It's a place where education and entertainment come together, making it an ideal destination for visitors of all ages.

The zoo offers various exhibits, including Teton Trek, a nod to the Greater Yellowstone ecosystem, and the Zambezi River Hippo Camp, where you can watch hippos both above and below the water. There's also a Giant Panda exhibit that is particularly popular. The zoo has invested in creating an environment that's both enriching for the animals and informative for visitors.

Memphis Zoo is not just about observing animals; it's also deeply involved in conservation efforts and education. It's an opportunity to connect with wildlife and understand the importance of protecting our planet's diverse species.

7. Shelby Farms Park

Address: 6903 Great View Drive North, Memphis, TN 38134
Shelby Farms Park is a gem within the city, boasting the title of one of the largest urban parks in the United States. It's a haven for outdoor enthusiasts, offering a wide range of activities and green spaces to explore.

The park features miles of hiking and biking trails that wind through lush forests and open meadows. There's a beautiful lake where you can rent paddleboats or canoes for a relaxing afternoon on the water. If you're up for an adventure, there's a treetop adventure course that offers ziplining and other challenging activities.

Families can enjoy the Woodland Discovery Playground, a massive play area with interactive features for kids of all ages. The park also hosts various events and programs, from yoga classes to bird watching.

Shelby Farms Park is a testament to Memphis' commitment to preserving green spaces and providing a place for residents and visitors to connect with nature.

8. Memphis Botanic Garden

Address: 750 Cherry Rd, Memphis, TN 38117

The Memphis Botanic Garden is a serene oasis within the city. It features 96 acres of beautifully landscaped gardens that provide a peaceful escape from the hustle and bustle of daily life. The gardens are meticulously maintained and offer a variety of experiences for visitors.

One of the highlights is the Japanese Garden, a tranquil space with a koi pond and stone lanterns that create a sense of serenity. The Rose Garden showcases a stunning collection of roses in full bloom during the spring and early summer. The Butterfly Garden is a delightful spot to observe these colorful insects.

For families, the Children's Garden is a favorite. It's an interactive area where kids can explore, learn, and have fun. There's even a giant treehouse for little adventurers.

The Memphis Botanic Garden often hosts seasonal events and exhibitions, making it a destination that changes with the seasons. It's a place where you can immerse yourself in the beauty of nature and find moments of tranquility.

9. Mud Island River Park

Address: 125 N Front St, Memphis, TN 38103
Mud Island River Park is a unique and engaging attraction situated on the Mississippi River. The park's centerpiece is the Riverwalk model, a detailed replica of the lower Mississippi River, complete with flowing water. You can follow the model's path while learning about the history and geography of the river.

One of the most popular activities at Mud Island is taking pedal boats out on the Riverwalk. It's a fun and leisurely way to explore the replica river and take in scenic views of the Mississippi. In the summer, the park hosts the "Mud Island

River Park Summer Concert Series," featuring live music on a floating stage.

Mud Island River Park also houses the Mississippi River Museum, where you can delve deeper into the history, culture, and ecology of the Mississippi River. The museum features a range of interactive exhibits and artifacts.

The park's amphitheater, known as Mud Island Amphitheatre, hosts live concerts and events, offering a unique venue with the Mississippi River as the backdrop.

Mud Island River Park is a blend of education, entertainment, and natural beauty, making it a great destination for families and those interested in river history.

10. Memphis Rock 'n' Soul Museum

Address: 191 Beale St, Memphis, TN 38103
The Memphis Rock 'n' Soul Museum, affiliated with the Smithsonian Institution, tells the story of the birth of rock and soul music. It's located on Beale Street, in the heart of Memphis' music scene.

The museum's exhibits are a journey through the history of music in Memphis, exploring the cultural influences that gave rise to rock 'n' roll and soul music. Visitors can expect to see a wide array of artifacts, from early blues recordings to Elvis Presley's first Sun Studio sessions. Interactive exhibits and audiovisual presentations enhance the experience, offering a deep understanding of how Memphis played a pivotal role in shaping the music industry.

The museum is divided into seven galleries, each covering a different aspect of Memphis music history, from the rural roots of the blues to the birth of soul music on the streets of

Memphis. It provides insight into the contributions of artists like B.B. King, Howlin' Wolf, and Johnny Cash.

The Memphis Rock 'n' Soul Museum is a place where you can immerse yourself in the musical tapestry of Memphis and understand how this city influenced the world's most popular genres.

11. Grind City Brewing Company

Address: 76 Waterworks Ave, Memphis, TN 38107
For beer enthusiasts, a visit to Grind City Brewing Company is a delightful experience. Located in the revitalized Uptown neighborhood of Memphis, this local brewery offers a range of craft beers that reflect the spirit of the city.

The brewery has a relaxed and welcoming atmosphere, making it a great place to unwind with friends or make new acquaintances. You can take a brewery tour to learn about the brewing process and the history of Grind City Brewing. The knowledgeable staff is always eager to share their passion for beer and Memphis culture.

Grind City Brewing Company's beer selection includes a variety of styles, from IPAs to stouts, ensuring there's something for every palate. The brewery often hosts events, live music, and food trucks, creating a vibrant social scene.

It's not just about the beer; it's about experiencing Memphis' burgeoning craft beer scene and getting a taste of the local culture.

12. Memphis Riverboats

Address: 251 Riverside Dr, Memphis, TN 38103

Exploring the mighty Mississippi River aboard one of the Memphis Riverboats is an experience that combines history, entertainment, and stunning scenery. The riverboats offer various cruise options, ensuring there's something for every type of visitor.

The most popular cruise is the Memphis Sightseeing Cruise, which provides a narrated tour of the river, sharing fascinating tales of Memphis' history and the importance of the Mississippi. There are also specialty cruises, including dinner cruises with live music and themed events.

The views of Memphis from the river are captivating, with the city's skyline and iconic landmarks like the Pyramid and Tom Lee Park in the backdrop. It's a serene and refreshing way to see the city from a unique perspective.

Memphis Riverboats often incorporate live music into their cruises, offering a taste of the city's musical heritage as you float along the Mississippi. Whether you're interested in history, relaxation, or a romantic evening, a riverboat cruise is a must-do activity in Memphis.

13. Mississippi River Park

Address: Riverside Dr, Memphis, TN 38103
The Mississippi River Park is a picturesque stretch of green space along the banks of the mighty Mississippi River. It's a peaceful and scenic area where you can take leisurely strolls, enjoy a picnic, or simply soak in the beauty of the river.

The park offers stunning views of the Mississippi River and the Hernando de Soto Bridge, creating a serene atmosphere for relaxation and reflection. It's a popular spot for locals and visitors to watch riverboats and barges traveling along the river.

As you explore the park, you'll come across beautiful sculptures, walking paths, and benches where you can sit and take in the tranquil surroundings. The Mississippi River Park is especially charming during sunrise and sunset when the river's reflections are at their most captivating.

It's a simple yet enchanting destination, providing a peaceful escape from the city's bustling energy.

14. Dixon Gallery and Gardens

Address: 4339 Park Ave, Memphis, TN 38117
The Dixon Gallery and Gardens is an art museum housed in a beautiful mansion set within 17 acres of lush gardens. It's an ideal destination for art enthusiasts and nature lovers alike.

The mansion itself is a work of art, featuring elegant architecture and interior design. The galleries within the museum showcase a remarkable collection of European and American art, including works by Monet, Renoir, and Degas. The museum often hosts traveling exhibitions, providing a dynamic and ever-changing cultural experience.

The gardens surrounding the museum are a highlight. You'll find a wide variety of plants, including roses, camellias, and magnolias. There's a koi pond, a woodland garden, and a cutting garden. The gardens are meticulously maintained and offer a tranquil space for contemplation and relaxation.

The Dixon Gallery and Gardens often host special events, educational programs, and family-friendly activities. It's a destination that combines art, culture, and the beauty of nature in a single location.

15. Metal Museum

Address: 374 Metal Museum Dr, Memphis, TN 38106
The Metal Museum is a unique and niche attraction that focuses on the art of metalworking and sculpture. It's located on the grounds of the historic Ulysses S. Grant's mansion, offering a stunning riverside location.

The museum houses an extensive collection of metalwork, including both historical and contemporary pieces. Visitors can explore various exhibitions that showcase the diversity of metal as an artistic medium. The museum often features pieces from both renowned and emerging metal artists.

The Metal Museum is not just about viewing art; it's a place of hands-on learning and engagement. The museum offers workshops and classes in metalworking, allowing visitors to try their hand at blacksmithing, casting, and other metal-related crafts. These educational opportunities make the Metal Museum an interactive and immersive experience.

The outdoor sculpture garden is a tranquil space where visitors can admire large-scale metal sculptures set against the backdrop of the Mississippi River. It's a unique blend of art, history, and craftsmanship.

16. Grizzlies' NBA Game at FedExForum

Address: 191 Beale St, Memphis, TN 38103
If you're a sports enthusiast, attending an NBA game featuring the Memphis Grizzlies at the FedExForum is an electrifying experience. The arena is a lively hub of basketball action, known for its passionate fan base and energetic atmosphere. Cheering for the home team and watching world-class athletes in action is an unforgettable Memphis experience.

The FedExForum also hosts concerts, college basketball games, and other entertainment events, making it a versatile venue that offers something for everyone.

17. Sunken Historical Monuments in Mississippi River Park

Address: Riverside Dr, Memphis, TN 38103
Just south of the Mississippi River Park, you'll find a unique and lesser-known attraction. During the low-water period in the late summer and fall, when the river's levels drop, historic riverboat wrecks and other remnants become visible. These sunken historical monuments provide a glimpse into the past, showcasing artifacts and structures that have been submerged for many years. It's a fascinating opportunity for history buffs and those intrigued by the river's history.

18. Slave Haven Underground Railroad Museum

Address: 826 N. Second St., Memphis, TN 38107
Memphis played a significant role in the Underground Railroad, and the Slave Haven Underground Railroad Museum, also known as the Burkle Estate, is a testament to that history. The house, once owned by Jacob Burkle, served as a station for escaping slaves on their journey to freedom.

Guided tours take you through secret passageways, trapdoors, and hidden compartments used by freedom seekers. You'll gain insights into the perilous journey and the courage of those who risked their lives for freedom. It's a compelling and educational experience that sheds light on a crucial chapter in American history.

19. The Cotton Museum

Address: 65 Union Ave, Memphis, TN 38103

Memphis' history is deeply entwined with the cotton industry, and the Cotton Museum is the place to explore this heritage. The museum is housed in the historic Memphis Cotton Exchange building, and it offers a comprehensive look at the cotton industry's impact on the city and the South.

The exhibits feature artifacts, interactive displays, and multimedia presentations that highlight the history of cotton farming, ginning, and trading. You'll also learn about the cultural and economic significance of cotton in the region. The Cotton Museum provides a deeper understanding of Memphis' roots and its role in the cotton industry.

20. Memphis Pyramid (Bass Pro Shops at the Pyramid)

Address: 1 Bass Pro Dr, Memphis, TN 38105

The Memphis Pyramid, originally a sports and entertainment venue, has been transformed into a one-of-a-kind retail and entertainment destination, thanks to Bass Pro Shops. The massive pyramid structure now houses an indoor swamp, an artificial cypress swamp, an enormous retail store, a bowling alley, a hotel, and several restaurants.

One of the most remarkable features is the freestanding elevator that takes visitors to the top of the pyramid, offering breathtaking views of the Mississippi River and downtown Memphis. It's a unique and quirky attraction that combines shopping, dining, and adventure.

21. Memphis Brooks Museum of Art

Address: 1934 Poplar Ave, Memphis, TN 38104

The Memphis Brooks Museum of Art is the oldest and largest art museum in Tennessee. The museum's collection features an impressive array of art, including European and American works, contemporary art, and African art. It's a cultural treasure trove that showcases a diverse range of artistic styles and periods.

The museum often hosts special exhibitions and educational programs, making it a dynamic and engaging place for art enthusiasts. The serene and spacious galleries create a relaxing atmosphere for contemplation and appreciation of art.

22. Pink Palace Museum

Address: 3050 Central Ave, Memphis, TN 38111
The Pink Palace Museum is a remarkable cultural and historical institution in Memphis. It offers a wide range of exhibits, including natural history, cultural history, and a planetarium. The museum's most famous exhibit is the Clyde Parke Miniature Circus, a detailed miniature replica of a circus that took over 40 years to complete.

The museum also houses the historic Pink Palace mansion, which was once the home of the founder of Piggly Wiggly, a groundbreaking self-service grocery store chain. The mansion is a stunning example of the Spanish Colonial Revival style and provides insights into the lifestyle of the early 20th century elite.

The Pink Palace Museum is an educational and entertaining destination for families, history buffs, and those curious about the world around them.

23. Elmwood Cemetery

Address: 824 S. Dudley St, Memphis, TN 38104
Elmwood Cemetery is a historic cemetery that provides a fascinating glimpse into Memphis' past. It's the final resting place of many influential figures in the city's history, including politicians, soldiers, and notable citizens.

The cemetery's beautiful landscape, with winding paths, mature trees, and ornate tombstones, creates a serene and reflective environment. Guided tours are available, shedding light on the history and stories of those buried in Elmwood.

Elmwood Cemetery is a place of historical significance, peaceful contemplation, and natural beauty.

24. Memphis Farmers Market

Address: G.E. Patterson Ave & S. Front St, Memphis, TN 38103
If you're visiting Memphis on a Saturday morning, don't miss the Memphis Farmers Market. It's a vibrant gathering of local farmers, artisans, and food producers. The market showcases fresh produce, artisanal products, handcrafted goods, and delicious street food.

It's not only a place to shop for locally sourced items but also an opportunity to engage with the Memphis community and experience the city's culinary diversity. Live music often accompanies the market, creating a lively and festive atmosphere.

The Memphis Farmers Market provides a taste of the city's vibrant food culture and an opportunity to support local businesses.

25. Overton Park

Address: 1914 Poplar Ave, Memphis, TN 38104

Overton Park is a sprawling urban oasis in the heart of Memphis. It offers a wide range of attractions and activities, making it a popular destination for locals and visitors alike.

The park is home to the Memphis Brooks Museum of Art, the Memphis Zoo, and the Memphis College of Art. You'll also find the Memphis Brooks Museum of Art and the Memphis College of Art within the park's borders. The Memphis Brooks Museum of Art is the oldest and largest art museum in Tennessee, while the Memphis College of Art contributes to the park's creative and educational atmosphere.

Overton Park is also known for its beautiful greenspaces, including the Old Forest State Natural Area, a unique urban old-growth forest. The Levitt Shell, an outdoor amphitheater, hosts free concerts and events throughout the year. The park provides ample space for picnics, sports, and leisurely walks.

Whether you're interested in culture, nature, or relaxation, Overton Park has something to offer everyone. It's a central gathering place for Memphians and a beloved part of the city's identity.

Memphis is a city of multifaceted charm, offering a diverse range of attractions that cater to varied interests. These additional examples showcase the city's rich history, culture, and natural beauty, ensuring that every visitor finds something captivating and unique in this vibrant Tennessee metropolis. Whether you're exploring historical sites or indulging in art, music, or outdoor adventures, Memphis is a city that welcomes all with open arms.

Gastronomic Delight & Entertainment

Best local Cuisine to try out

Memphis is renowned for its mouthwatering culinary traditions. When you're visiting Memphis, you can't miss out on the chance to savor some of the best local cuisine. From finger-licking barbecue to soulful comfort food, Memphis offers a gastronomic journey that's hard to forget. Here, we'll explore some of the must-try dishes and restaurants to experience the full flavor of Memphis.

1. BBQ Ribs:

Memphis is often referred to as the "Barbecue Capital of the World," and the city's barbecue ribs are a testament to this title. When in Memphis, you must indulge in some succulent, slow-cooked, and perfectly seasoned ribs. The city is known for its two distinct styles of barbecue: dry-rubbed and wet sauce. Charlie Vergos' Rendezvous and Central BBQ are two iconic places to sample these delectable ribs. Whether you prefer your ribs coated in a flavorful dry rub or dripping with mouthwatering sauce, you won't be disappointed.

2. Pulled Pork Sandwich:

Another barbecue delight, the pulled pork sandwich, is a local favorite in Memphis. Tender, slow-cooked pulled pork is piled onto a soft bun and topped with a dollop of coleslaw for that perfect combination of savory and tangy. Gus's World Famous Fried Chicken is an excellent place to experience this dish, along with their legendary fried chicken. The combination of the two is a real treat for your taste buds.

3. Hot Tamales:

You might be surprised to discover that Memphis has its own version of hot tamales, a dish with deep Mississippi Delta roots. These hot tamales are small, spicy, and traditionally made with seasoned ground beef, wrapped in corn husks. A local institution known for serving up these flavorful treats is the "Four Way," a classic soul food restaurant that's been dishing out Southern comfort food for generations.

4. Grits:

Grits are a Southern staple, and Memphis is no exception. Creamy and hearty, these ground corn porridge is the ideal comfort food. Whether you prefer them cheesy or served with shrimp and gravy, you'll find various versions to satisfy your taste buds at local eateries such as Arcade Restaurant, the oldest café in Memphis.

5. Fried Catfish:

Being in a city situated on the Mississippi River, it's no wonder that fried catfish is a popular dish in Memphis. The local restaurants serve up this crispy and golden delight, often accompanied by hushpuppies and coleslaw. Try it at Soul Fish Café, where you can enjoy this Southern classic served to perfection.

6. Banana Pudding:

After indulging in savory dishes, save room for dessert, and try Memphis' iconic banana pudding. It's a creamy and sweet concoction of bananas, vanilla wafers, and vanilla pudding. Locals know it's a dessert that warms the soul, and one of the best places to enjoy it is at The Cupboard Restaurant.

7. Soul Food:

Memphis is a city that boasts an enduring love for soul food. The cuisine is characterized by hearty, rich, and comforting dishes, often rooted in African American culinary traditions.

The Four Way, mentioned earlier, is a standout example of a place where you can savor soul food classics like smothered pork chops, fried chicken, and collard greens.

8. Muddy's Bake Shop:
If you have a sweet tooth, Muddy's Bake Shop is a must-visit. They offer a delightful selection of cakes, pies, and cookies, all made with love and the finest ingredients. Be sure to try their Prozac Cake, a heavenly blend of chocolate, peanut butter, and more.

9. BBQ Nachos:
You may think you've had nachos before, but have you tried Memphis BBQ nachos? They're a unique and mouthwatering creation, featuring barbecue pork or chicken piled high on tortilla chips, smothered in cheese and topped with jalapeños. Central BBQ serves up some of the best BBQ nachos in town.

10. Beale Street Restaurants:
Beale Street is not just famous for its live music but also for its diverse culinary offerings. While exploring this iconic street, you can sample a wide range of Memphis's culinary delights. Whether it's at Silky O'Sullivan's for their famous Diver Bucket cocktail and lamb fries or Rum Boogie Café for their signature Soul Burger, you won't be disappointed.

11. Memphis-style Pizza:
While Memphis isn't as famous for pizza as cities like New York or Chicago, it has its own unique style worth trying. Memphis-style pizza often features a cracker-thin crust, a sweet and tangy tomato sauce, and a generous amount of cheese. Try it at local pizzerias like Coletta's or Rock'N Dough Pizza Co.

12. Fried Chicken:

In addition to the renowned Gus's World Famous Fried Chicken, Memphis offers many other fantastic places to enjoy this Southern classic. Other notable spots include Uncle Lou's Fried Chicken and Willie Moore's Restaurant. The crispy, juicy, and flavorful fried chicken will leave you craving for more.

13. Cornbread:

Cornbread is a Southern staple and a must-try when in Memphis. It's often served as a side dish with meals and comes in various forms, from sweet and moist to savory and crumbly. Local restaurants like Alcenia's and The Beauty Shop serve up delicious cornbread that perfectly complements their main dishes.

14. Po' Boys:

While traditionally associated with New Orleans, you can find some amazing Po' Boys in Memphis as well. These sandwiches are usually stuffed with fried seafood, roast beef, or other savory fillings. Try the Memphis twist on this classic at restaurants like Soul Fish Café and The Second Line.

15. Sweet Tea:

No Southern meal is complete without a glass of sweet tea. Memphis offers sweet tea that's the perfect blend of sugar and iced tea, making it a refreshing and satisfying beverage to accompany your meal. You can find sweet tea at nearly every restaurant in the city.

16. Collard Greens:

Collard greens are a quintessential Southern side dish. They're slow-cooked with flavorful ingredients like ham hocks or bacon, resulting in tender and savory greens. Many local eateries serve delicious collard greens to accompany your main course.

17. Hot Chicken:
While hot chicken is famously associated with Nashville, Memphis also offers its version of this spicy delight. If you're a fan of spicy food, be sure to try the hot chicken at places like Hattie B's Hot Chicken or Gus's World Famous Fried Chicken, which offers both hot and mild options.

18. Banana's Foster:
For a sweet and decadent dessert, consider trying Banana's Foster. This dessert is typically made by flambéing sliced bananas in a rich, buttery, and rum-infused sauce. Many upscale restaurants in Memphis offer this delightful treat to end your meal on a high note.

19. Meat and Three:
The "Meat and Three" concept is a Southern tradition, and Memphis has its own take on it. You choose a meat (like fried chicken, catfish, or pork chops) and three side dishes (often including mashed potatoes, mac and cheese, green beans, and more). Arnold's BBQ and Grill is one spot to enjoy a hearty Meat and Three meal.

20. Fried Pickles:
Fried pickles are a delightful appetizer or snack that you can find at various local restaurants and bars. These crispy, tangy treats are often served with a dipping sauce and make for a perfect complement to your meal or as a standalone snack.

In addition to these specific dishes, Memphis is known for its food festivals and events that celebrate its rich food culture. The World Championship Barbecue Cooking Contest, held annually in May, is a great opportunity to taste some of the finest barbecue dishes Memphis has to offer.

When you visit Memphis, you'll experience not just the vibrant culture and music but also the incredible food that makes this city truly special. Be sure to explore the local cuisine, try some or all of the dishes mentioned above, and savor the rich flavors of Memphis, a city that knows how to satisfy the soul through the stomach. From barbecue to soul food, and everything in between, Memphis is a culinary delight that you won't want to miss. So, prepare your taste buds for a flavor-filled adventure and enjoy the best local cuisine Memphis has to offer.

Best Local Drinks to try Out

Memphis, Tennessee, is not only known for its rich musical heritage and mouthwatering barbecue, but it's also a city that boasts a vibrant and diverse drinking scene. Whether you're a fan of classic cocktails, craft beer, or unique local concoctions, Memphis has something to quench every thirst. When you find yourself in the birthplace of the blues and home to Graceland, make sure to try these best local drinks that encapsulate the spirit of Memphis.

Beale Street Brews
When in Memphis, a visit to Beale Street is almost obligatory. Known as the "Home of the Blues," this iconic street is not only a hub for music but also for some fantastic local beverages. Beale Street Brews are a collection of craft beers that capture the essence of this historic street. From the light and crisp Wheat Ale to the robust and flavorful Beale Street Stout, these brews offer the perfect accompaniment to live music and vibrant street life.

Memphis Mule
A southern twist on the classic Moscow Mule, the Memphis Mule is a delightful blend of vodka, ginger beer, and fresh lime juice, served in a frosty copper mug. It's a refreshing

and zesty drink that can help you beat the Memphis heat while exploring the city.

Pickleback Shot
For the more adventurous drinkers, the Pickleback Shot is a Memphis tradition. This unusual pairing consists of a shot of whiskey followed by a shot of pickle brine. It might sound strange, but the tangy pickle juice effectively cuts through the whiskey's bite, creating a unique and surprisingly tasty combination.

Memphis Blues Martini
Memphis is synonymous with blues music, and the Memphis Blues Martini pays homage to this musical heritage. This cocktail combines blueberry vodka, blue curaçao, and fresh lemon juice to create a vibrant and visually striking drink that's as smooth as a blues riff.

Gus's World-Famous Bloody Mary
Gus's World-Famous Fried Chicken is an iconic eatery in Memphis, known for its mouthwatering fried chicken. But they also serve a mean Bloody Mary. It's a hearty concoction with a secret recipe mix, topped with pickles, olives, and other garnishes that make it a meal in a glass.

Sweet Tea Vodka
Memphis and the South are famous for their sweet tea, and what better way to elevate this beloved beverage than by adding a generous dose of sweet tea-flavored vodka. This drink is often served simply over ice or with a splash of lemonade for a delightful summer sipper.

Memphis Craft Beer
Memphis has seen a surge in craft breweries in recent years. There are numerous options for beer enthusiasts to explore local flavors and unique brews. Ghost River Brewing,

Wiseacre Brewing Co., and High Cotton Brewing Co. are just a few of the establishments that offer a wide range of craft beer choices. Whether you prefer a hoppy IPA, a rich stout, or a crisp lager, Memphis has something for every palate.

Southern Comfort

No visit to Memphis would be complete without a taste of Southern Comfort. This famous American whiskey liqueur was created in New Orleans but has deep southern roots. It's a sweet and smooth spirit that can be enjoyed straight or in cocktails like the Southern Comfort Sour or the Memphis Sweet Tea.

Old Dominick Distillery Cocktails

The Old Dominick Distillery, located in the heart of downtown Memphis, is a historic establishment that has been revived to produce high-quality spirits. You can enjoy tours of the distillery and sample their exceptional whiskey, vodka, and gin in a variety of cocktails created by their expert mixologists. The rooftop bar offers stunning views of the Mississippi River and the city skyline, making it an ideal spot to relax and savor the local flavors.

Walking in Memphis

For a truly unique local experience, try the "Walking in Memphis" cocktail. It's a blend of bourbon, amaretto, and fresh lemon juice, served in a glass rimmed with crushed graham crackers. This drink encapsulates the flavors of the city, from the warmth of the bourbon to the subtle sweetness of amaretto, with a hint of tangy lemon.

Loflin Yard's Signature Cocktails

Loflin Yard is an oasis in the city, offering a rustic and laid-back ambiance with a diverse menu of signature cocktails. You can enjoy a "Hemingway in Memphis" (a twist on the classic Hemingway Daiquiri) or the "Memphis Thyme" with gin, thyme-infused syrup, and citrus, among others. The serene outdoor setting with fire pits and live music makes it a must-visit destination.

The Memphis Belle

Named after the famous WWII bomber, The Memphis Belle is a classic cocktail with a regional twist. It combines bourbon, elderflower liqueur, fresh lemon juice, and a splash of club soda. It's a light, refreshing, and slightly floral drink that's perfect for sipping on a warm Memphis day.

Grindhouse Killer Burgers' Milkshakes

Grindhouse Killer Burgers, a local favorite for burgers and milkshakes, offers some exceptional adult milkshake options. They blend ice cream with spirits like bourbon, vodka, and Kahlúa to create indulgent and boozy shakes. The "S'mores" shake, with chocolate ice cream, marshmallow fluff, and bourbon, is a particular highlight.

Memphis Lemonade

This is a non-alcoholic beverage that's perfect for all ages. Memphis Lemonade is a refreshing combination of lemon juice, simple syrup, and club soda. You can find it in many eateries and restaurants throughout the city. It's the ideal drink for quenching your thirst during hot summer days.

Downtown Memphis Waterfront Punch

If you're strolling along the Mississippi River on a sunny day, consider sipping on some Downtown Memphis Waterfront Punch. This fruity and vibrant cocktail is typically made with a mix of fruit juices, rum, and a splash of grenadine, served over ice. It's a delightful drink to accompany the scenic riverfront views.

Memphis Coffee

After a day of exploring Graceland, Sun Studio, and the Stax Museum of American Soul Music, you might need a pick-me-up. Memphis Coffee, a hot drink with a kick, is the answer. It's a blend of hot coffee, Irish cream liqueur, and cinnamon whiskey, often garnished with whipped cream and a dash of cinnamon. It's perfect for keeping the energy going while experiencing the city's rich cultural heritage.

Local Fruit Juices

Memphis and the surrounding region are abundant in fresh, locally grown fruits. You'll find a variety of juice bars and cafes offering a selection of fruit juices and smoothies made from the freshest ingredients. Try the watermelon juice, pineapple-mint fusion, or blackberry blend to cool down and stay hydrated.

Bardog Tavern's Signature Drinks

Bardog Tavern is a popular local watering hole known for its signature cocktails. The "Dirty Diving Board" combines vodka, watermelon liqueur, and a splash of lemon juice, while the "Sweet Heat" is a spicy mix of tequila, jalapeño-infused agave, and lime. The creative libations at Bardog are sure to tantalize your taste buds.

Sun Studio Lemonade

When you visit Sun Studio, often dubbed the "Birthplace of Rock 'n' Roll," don't forget to order a Sun Studio Lemonade. This citrusy concoction is a blend of lemonade, lime juice, and a hint of grenadine. It's a tribute to the legendary musicians who recorded their hits in this historic studio.

Memphis Mint Julep

The Mint Julep is a classic Southern cocktail, and Memphis has its own twist on this iconic drink. It features bourbon, fresh mint leaves, and a dash of simple syrup, served in a chilled glass. The combination of the cool mint and the warmth of the bourbon makes for a soothing and traditional Southern sipper.

Memphis Rooftop Bar Specials
Memphis boasts several rooftop bars that offer stunning views of the cityscape. Many of these bars have their own unique drink specials that cater to a variety of tastes. Enjoy a cocktail while taking in the breathtaking scenery from one of these elevated establishments.

Goner Records Beer
For those with a taste for vinyl and a love for music, Goner Records is a must-visit shop in Memphis. In addition to its extensive vinyl collection, Goner Records also collaborates with local breweries to produce limited-edition craft beers. These beers often feature custom label art, and they make for excellent souvenirs to take home with you.

Taste of Memphis Flight
If you're indecisive or simply want to sample a variety of local beverages, consider ordering a "Taste of Memphis" flight. Many bars and restaurants in Memphis offer these flights, which typically include a selection of the city's signature cocktails, beers, and other libations. It's an excellent way to get a well-rounded experience of Memphis's drink culture.

Memphis Blue Lagoon
A dazzling blue cocktail known as the "Memphis Blue Lagoon" is a visual and flavorful delight. Made with blue curaçao, vodka, lemonade, and a splash of club soda, this drink is reminiscent of the city's musical heritage, mixing vibrant colors and upbeat flavors.

Choose Your Own Adventure

Finally, one of the best ways to explore Memphis's drink scene is to embark on a "Choose Your Own Adventure" night. This approach involves hopping from one bar or restaurant to another, trying their signature drinks, and soaking up the city's unique ambiance. By doing so, you'll not only discover some hidden gems but also engage with the local culture and people.

From traditional Southern classics to creative and modern concoctions, there's a drink to suit every palate. Whether you're sipping a Memphis Mule on Beale Street, enjoying craft beer at a local brewery, or savoring a Memphis Blue Lagoon in a rooftop bar, you're sure to find a drink that captures the heart and soul of this vibrant and musical city. So, raise your glass and toast to Memphis, where the music, food, and drinks harmonize to create a one-of-a-kind experience.

Top Restaurant

Memphis has more to offer than just its music history. Memphis is a melting pot of diverse cultures and flavors, making it a food lover's paradise. When visiting this vibrant city, exploring the local and intercontinental dishes at some of its top restaurants is a must. we will take you on a culinary journey through Memphis, showcasing the best places to savor mouthwatering local and intercontinental dishes, along with their addresses.

Gus's World Famous Fried Chicken

Address: 310 S Front St, Memphis, TN 38103

Signature Dish: The must-try dish at Gus's is, of course, their world-famous fried chicken. It's known for its perfectly crispy exterior and tender, juicy interior. What sets Gus's apart is their secret spice blend, which adds a unique kick to the chicken, making it one of the best fried chicken spots in Memphis.

What Makes It Special: The unassuming, no-frills atmosphere and the consistently fantastic fried chicken are what make Gus's special. Whether you prefer it spicy or mild, the flavor is unmatched, and the experience is quintessentially Memphis.

The Rendezvous

Address: 52 S 2nd St, Memphis, TN 38103

Signature Dish: The Rendezvous is famous for its dry-rubbed ribs. These ribs are slow-cooked to perfection, resulting in fall-off-the-bone tenderness. The dry rub, with a blend of spices, gives the ribs a unique flavor that's unforgettable.

What Makes It Special: The Rendezvous is an iconic barbecue joint in Memphis, and it's not just about the food. The atmosphere, located in a historic basement, adds to the charm. It's a piece of history where you can enjoy mouthwatering barbecue.

Cozy Corner

Address: 735 N Pkwy, Memphis, TN 38105

Signature Dish: Cozy Corner's claim to fame is its Cornish game hen. This dish features a tender and flavorful hen that's slow-cooked to perfection. The secret sauce is the key to its distinctive flavor.

What Makes It Special: Cozy Corner's modest exterior hides a culinary gem. The welcoming atmosphere and the dedication to creating mouthwatering barbecue dishes, particularly the Cornish game hen, make it a beloved spot for locals and visitors alike.

Central BBQ

Address: 2249 Central Ave, Memphis, TN 38104

Signature Dish: Central BBQ offers a variety of barbecue dishes, but their pulled pork sandwiches are a local favorite. The tender, smoky pulled pork is served on a fluffy bun, and you can add their signature sauces for an extra kick.

What Makes It Special: Central BBQ is known for its diverse menu, quality smoked meats, and its range of sauces. Whether you're a fan of pulled pork, ribs, or smoked sausage, Central BBQ has something for everyone.

Flight Restaurant and Wine Bar

Address: 39 S Main St, Memphis, TN 38103

Signature Dish: Flight Restaurant and Wine Bar is unique in that it offers flights of various dishes. This allows you to sample different flavors in one meal. Whether it's seafood, steak, or international cuisine, you can mix and match your favorites.

What Makes It Special: The concept of serving flights of dishes makes Flight Restaurant and Wine Bar a standout. It's perfect for adventurous eaters who want to explore a variety of flavors in one dining experience. Their extensive wine selection complements the food beautifully.

Babalu Tacos & Tapas

Address: 2115 Madison Ave, Memphis, TN 38104

Signature Dish: Babalu is known for its Babalu Tacos, which are filled with flavorful ingredients. The handmade tortillas and creative fillings make for a delightful combination. Don't forget to start your meal with their signature guacamole.

What Makes It Special: Babalu offers a fusion of international and local flavors in a trendy setting. The variety of tacos and tapas, as well as the handcrafted cocktails, make it a go-to spot for those looking for a contemporary dining experience.

These restaurants showcase the rich culinary diversity of Memphis, from classic Southern barbecue joints to modern, fusion-inspired eateries. Whether you're in the mood for traditional Memphis flavors or want to explore international tastes, the city has something to satisfy every palate.

Best bar and Cafe in the city

1. Beale Street:

Beale Street is often dubbed as the "Home of the Blues" and is an iconic entertainment district known for its vibrant nightlife. This historic street is filled with a variety of bars, live music venues, and restaurants that cater to a wide range of tastes. As you stroll down Beale Street, you'll be serenaded by the soulful sounds of blues music and encounter a diverse crowd of locals and tourists.

Silky O'Sullivan's: Silky O'Sullivan's is a Beale Street staple that's famous for its lively atmosphere and unique frozen drinks. One of the standout features is their "Diver," a massive, shareable cocktail served in a large bucket-like glass. This establishment is also known for its resident dueling pianos, which entertain patrons while they enjoy their drinks.

B.B. King's Blues Club: Named in honor of the legendary blues musician B.B. King, this club is a music lover's paradise. You can experience top-notch live blues performances here while indulging in delicious Southern cuisine. Their menu includes mouthwatering dishes like gumbo, catfish, and, of course, finger-licking barbecue.

Rum Boogie Café: The Rum Boogie Café is another iconic stop on Beale Street, famous for its extensive rum collection and fantastic live music. The cafe is a cozy and inviting space with a memorabilia-rich interior that adds to the overall ambiance. While you sip on your favorite rum cocktail, you can enjoy live blues and rock 'n' roll performances.

2. Gus's World Famous Fried Chicken:

Gus's World Famous Fried Chicken is a true Memphis institution. Located at 310 S Front St, this unassuming eatery serves some of the best fried chicken you'll ever taste. The recipe for their crispy, golden-brown chicken has been a closely guarded secret for generations, and the result is a mouthwatering, spicy, and perfectly fried chicken that's juicy on the inside and crispy on the outside. The moment you bite into a piece, you'll understand why it's considered world-famous.

What sets Gus's apart is not just their exceptional chicken but also the sides that accompany it. You can enjoy classics like mac 'n' cheese, baked beans, coleslaw, and more. The combination of the succulent chicken and these delightful sides creates a satisfying and memorable dining experience.

3. Otherlands Coffee Bar:

If you're a coffee lover or simply in need of a cozy spot to relax, Otherlands Coffee Bar is the place to be. Nestled at 641 S Cooper St, this eclectic and welcoming cafe offers a diverse range of coffee options, teas, and delectable baked goods. The interior is a fusion of colors and artwork that creates an artsy and unique atmosphere. It's not just a place to enjoy a cup of coffee; it's a hub for the local community.

The coffee menu includes classics like espresso, cappuccino, and pour-over, as well as a variety of specialty drinks. Whether you prefer your coffee black and bold or adorned with flavorful syrups and frothy milk, Otherlands can accommodate your preferences. They also have an array of teas, both hot and iced, for those who aren't coffee enthusiasts.

The baked goods at Otherlands are just as impressive as the coffee. Their pastries, muffins, and cookies are baked fresh daily, ensuring that every treat you enjoy is at its peak of deliciousness. You can pair your coffee with a buttery croissant, a moist blueberry muffin, or a chocolate chip cookie that practically melts in your mouth.

4. Earnestine & Hazel's:

Earnestine & Hazel's, located at 531 S Main St, is a historic dive bar that embodies the soul of Memphis. This unpretentious gem is much more than just a bar; it's a time capsule of Memphis history and culture. As soon as you step inside, you'll be transported back in time as you take in the vintage decor, old jukeboxes, and a rich, authentic atmosphere that's uniquely Memphis.

One of the most famous items on the menu is the "Soul Burger." This burger is a legendary combination of a juicy beef patty, cheese, onions, pickles, and a secret sauce, all served on a classic bun. It's a must-try for anyone looking to experience Memphis's culinary heritage.

While Earnestine & Hazel's is primarily known as a bar, it's also reputed for its haunted history. The building is said to be haunted, and it's been featured in numerous paranormal investigations and documentaries. Whether you believe in ghosts or not, the stories and the ambiance make it a one-of-a-kind spot in Memphis.

5. Sun Studio Café:

For a taste of musical history along with your coffee or a quick bite, Sun Studio Café, situated at 706 Union Ave, is the perfect choice. This cafe is located inside the legendary Sun Studio, which holds a special place in music history. It's often referred to as the "Birthplace of Rock 'n' Roll" because of the famous artists who recorded there, including Elvis Presley, Johnny Cash, and Jerry Lee Lewis.

The walls of the cafe are adorned with music memorabilia and photographs that pay homage to the studio's iconic past. As you sip on your coffee, you can soak in the rich history of the place. The cafe offers a range of coffee drinks, from classic Americanos to specialty lattes, along with a selection of snacks and sandwiches to keep you energized during your visit.

Sun Studio Café is a must-visit for any music enthusiast, and it's an opportunity to connect with the roots of rock 'n' roll while enjoying a cup of joe.

6. High Cotton Brewing Co.:

High Cotton Brewing Co. at 598 Monroe Ave is a local craft brewery that's making waves in Memphis's growing craft beer scene. They take pride in brewing a variety of unique and flavorful beers, many of which are inspired by Memphis culture and traditions. The taproom at High Cotton is an excellent place to sample their brews and mingle with fellow beer enthusiasts.

The brewery's atmosphere is laid-back and welcoming, with a friendly and knowledgeable staff ready to guide you through their beer selection. They offer a diverse range of beer styles, from IPAs and stouts to seasonal and experimental brews. You can order a flight of different beers to explore the full spectrum of their offerings.

One of their most celebrated beers is the ESB (Extra Special Bitter), which is a well-balanced and flavorful beer that showcases their commitment to quality and craftsmanship. High Cotton Brewing Co. often hosts events and live music, so be sure to check their schedule for special happenings during your visit.

7. Barbecue Shop:

Memphis is famous for its barbecue, and one of the top places to experience authentic Memphis-style barbecue is the Barbecue Shop at 1782 Madison Ave. This unassuming, family-owned restaurant has been serving mouthwatering barbecue since 1985.

The Barbecue Shop is known for its succulent smoked ribs, which are tender and flavorful. The secret to their fantastic flavor is a dry rub that's applied before smoking the meat, resulting in a perfect balance of spices and smokiness. You can enjoy your ribs dry or wet, with the wet option featuring a tangy and delicious barbecue sauce.

In addition to ribs, the Barbecue Shop offers a variety of barbecue dishes, including pulled pork sandwiches, barbecue nachos, and barbecue spaghetti. The sides, such as coleslaw, baked beans, and potato salad, perfectly complement the main dishes and complete the classic Southern barbecue experience.

The restaurant's cozy and casual atmosphere is perfect for families and groups, and it's a beloved local spot that attracts barbecue enthusiasts from near and far.

8. Muddy's Bake Shop:

If you have a sweet tooth, Muddy's Bake Shop at 5101 Sanderlin Ave #114 will quickly become your go-to destination in Memphis. This charming bakery is celebrated for its delectable cakes, cookies, and cupcakes, all of which are lovingly made with top-quality ingredients and a lot of care.

The bakery's inviting interior, adorned with pastel colors and a vintage vibe, is a welcoming place to indulge in some of the most delightful sweet treats in Memphis. Their menu features an array of options, so whether you're in the mood for a slice of cake or a petite cookie, there's something for everyone.

Muddy's is known for its cupcakes, with flavors ranging from classic vanilla and chocolate to creative combinations like "Prozac," a chocolate cupcake filled with chocolate ganache and topped with chocolate buttercream. They also offer seasonal specials, so you'll have a variety to choose from based on the time of year.

Their baked goods are ideal for satisfying your sweet cravings or picking up a box of treats to share with friends and family. Muddy's Bake Shop is not just a bakery; it's a destination for celebrating life's sweet moments.

9. Railgarten:

Railgarten, located at 2166 Central Ave, is a truly unique establishment in Memphis. It combines elements of a bar, cafe, and outdoor entertainment space to offer visitors a multifaceted and fun experience. It's the kind of place where you can enjoy craft cocktails, coffee, and delicious food while playing a variety of games in the spacious outdoor area.

The indoor bar and cafe area of Railgarten is a comfortable and welcoming space with a retro-inspired decor. You can order a range of drinks, from well-crafted cocktails to a classic cup of coffee. The food menu includes a variety of tasty options, including sandwiches, salads, and snacks.

What sets Railgarten apart is its outdoor space, which features numerous games and activities. You can challenge your friends to a game of ping pong, shuffleboard, cornhole, or even volleyball. The atmosphere is lively, making it an ideal spot for group gatherings and fun-filled evenings. They also host regular live music events and other entertainment, so be sure to check their schedule for upcoming performances.

Railgarten's unique combination of indoor and outdoor spaces, along with its diverse menu and games, creates a memorable and entertaining experience for all who visit.

10. Blue Plate Café:

Blue Plate Café, located at 113 S Court Ave, is a classic Southern diner that offers hearty breakfast and lunch options. This quaint and cozy restaurant has been serving

Memphians for years and is known for its delicious, home-style dishes.

The menu at Blue Plate Café features a variety of Southern comfort food classics. If you're looking for a hearty breakfast, you can indulge in biscuits and gravy, country ham, and fluffy pancakes. The lunch options are equally satisfying, with dishes like meatloaf, fried catfish, and patty melts.

One of the highlights of dining at Blue Plate Café is the friendly and welcoming staff. The service here embodies the famous Southern hospitality, making you feel right at home as soon as you step through the door. The cozy atmosphere and comforting food make it a popular spot for locals and visitors alike.

Memphis is a city that combines the best of Southern culture, music, and culinary traditions. The bars and cafes mentioned in this guide are just a taste of what the city has to offer. Whether you're a music lover, a coffee connoisseur, a barbecue enthusiast, or a dessert fanatic, Memphis has a spot to satisfy your cravings and immerse you in its vibrant atmosphere.

From the iconic Beale Street with its live music venues and legendary bars to the unassuming but unforgettable Gus's World Famous Fried Chicken, and from the eclectic and community-driven Otherlands Coffee Bar to the time-capsule experience of Earnestine & Hazel's, Memphis offers a diverse array of places to explore.

If you want to connect with the city's musical heritage, you can't miss the Sun Studio Café. For craft beer enthusiasts, High Cotton Brewing Co. provides a great space to discover local brews. And if you're in Memphis for the barbecue, the Barbecue Shop has your ribs and pulled pork needs covered.

For those with a sweet tooth, Muddy's Bake Shop has an array of delightful treats, while Railgarten offers a unique blend of entertainment, food, and drinks. And when you're in the mood for a classic Southern diner experience, Blue Plate Café serves up comfort food with a smile.

As you visit these bars and cafes, you'll not only savor the flavors of Memphis but also immerse yourself in the culture and history of this incredible city. Memphis's unique blend of music, cuisine, and hospitality is sure to leave you with lasting memories and a desire to return for more.

Best Nightclub in the city

When you're in Memphis, you can't miss the opportunity to explore the city's nightlife, which boasts an array of nightclubs catering to diverse tastes and preferences. From iconic blues bars to modern dance clubs, Memphis has something for everyone. we'll take you through some of the best nightclubs in Memphis, complete with their addresses, so you can experience the city's nightlife at its finest.

Beale Street

Address: Beale St, Memphis, TN 38103
Beale Street is arguably the most famous nightclub destination in Memphis. It's a historic street known for its live music, neon signs, and an electrifying atmosphere. The street is lined with clubs, bars, and restaurants, making it a one-stop-shop for all your nightlife needs. Some of the renowned nightclubs on Beale Street include B.B. King's Blues Club, Rum Boogie Café, and Silky O'Sullivan's. Beale Street is the heart of Memphis nightlife and a must-visit for anyone looking to experience the city's vibrant music scene.

Lafayette's Music Room

Address: 2119 Madison Ave, Memphis, TN 38104

Lafayette's Music Room offers a unique blend of great music and fantastic food. Located in the heart of Overton Square, this venue is known for its live bands and musicians who perform a wide range of genres. The interior is cozy, creating an intimate atmosphere for you to enjoy the music while savoring some delicious Southern-inspired dishes.

Earnestine & Hazel's

Address: 531 S Main St, Memphis, TN 38103

If you're looking for a genuine dive bar experience with a touch of history, Earnestine & Hazel's is the place to be. This iconic spot in downtown Memphis was once a brothel and is now a beloved dive bar. The jukebox is packed with soulful tunes, and the upstairs area is even rumored to be haunted. It's a unique and memorable experience that you won't find anywhere else.

Electric Cowboy

Address: 6160 Macon Rd, Memphis, TN 38134

If you're into country music and line dancing, Electric Cowboy is the place to go. Located a bit outside downtown Memphis, this nightclub offers a fun and lively atmosphere with plenty of room for dancing. You can enjoy a variety of country hits while showing off your dance moves on the spacious dance floor.

Purple Haze Nightclub

Address: 140 Lt George W Lee Ave, Memphis, TN 38103

Purple Haze Nightclub is a vibrant and colorful venue that caters to lovers of hip-hop, EDM, and top 40 hits. With multiple bars and dance floors, it's a popular destination for those looking to dance the night away. The club often hosts themed parties and special events, so be sure to check their schedule for an exciting night out.

The Cove

Address: 2559 Broad Ave, Memphis, TN 38112
The Cove offers a unique experience with a tiki bar vibe. This retro-inspired nightclub is known for its craft cocktails and extensive rum selection. It's a great place to relax with friends and enjoy some of the best cocktails Memphis has to offer. They often have live music, adding to the laid-back atmosphere.

New Daisy Theatre

Address: 330 Beale St, Memphis, TN 38103
The New Daisy Theatre, located on Beale Street, is a historic venue that has hosted countless musical acts over the years. While it primarily serves as a concert venue, it also hosts nightclub events and dance parties. Check their schedule for upcoming events, and you might get the chance to dance the night away in this iconic setting.

Inferno Sports Bar and Grill

Address: 4859 Summer Ave, Memphis, TN 38122
For a sports-themed nightclub experience, Inferno Sports Bar and Grill is the place to be. This club features multiple TVs broadcasting live sports events, making it the ideal spot for sports enthusiasts. Enjoy your favorite drinks, delicious food, and even try your hand at a game of pool or darts.

Clayborn Temple

Address: 294 Hernando St, Memphis, TN 38126
The Clayborn Temple is a historic venue that often hosts unique nightlife events, including dance parties and live performances. This venue has a rich history and is a symbol

of the civil rights movement. It's worth checking their event schedule for a one-of-a-kind experience.

Club 152

Address: 152 Beale St, Memphis, TN 38103
Club 152 is another popular nightclub on Beale Street. Known for its high-energy dance floors, DJ sets, and diverse crowd, it's a great place to let loose and dance to your favorite tunes. The rooftop bar offers a fantastic view of the street below, making it a perfect spot to enjoy the nightlife.

Canvas
Address: 1737 Madison Ave, Memphis, TN 38104
Canvas is a modern and upscale nightclub located in the Midtown district of Memphis. It features a stylish interior, creative cocktails, and a trendy atmosphere. With regular DJ sets and themed parties, Canvas is the go-to spot for those who appreciate contemporary nightlife.

Mollie Fontaine Lounge

Address: 679 Adams Ave, Memphis, TN 38105
Housed in a beautiful historic mansion, Mollie Fontaine Lounge offers a unique nightlife experience. The lounge is known for its eclectic decor, craft cocktails, and live music. It's an intimate and charming venue that attracts a diverse crowd of locals and visitors.

Memphis is a city with a rich musical heritage, and its nightlife scene is a reflection of this heritage. Whether you're into blues, country, hip-hop, or electronic dance music, you'll find a nightclub that suits your tastes. Beale Street, in particular, is a must-visit, offering a variety of options in one convenient location.

Remember that nightclub hours, events, and offerings can change, so it's a good idea to check their websites or social media pages for the latest updates on hours of operation and special events. Additionally, be sure to respect local laws and drink responsibly while enjoying the nightlife in Memphis. No matter which nightclub you choose to explore, you're bound to have a memorable and entertaining night in this musical city.

Travel Itineraries

Family friendly itinerary

Here, we'll guide you through a perfect family trip to Memphis, including addresses and descriptions of must-visit places and activities. So, grab your travel checklist and get ready for a memorable experience in the "Home of the Blues."

Day 1: Arrival and Exploration of Downtown Memphis

Morning

Arrival at Memphis International Airport: Start your journey by landing at Memphis International Airport, located at 2491 Winchester Rd, Memphis, TN 38116. From here, you can easily access the city center.

Check-In at Your Accommodation: Memphis offers various family-friendly accommodations, including hotels, vacation rentals, and resorts. Choose one that suits your preferences and budget.

Lunch

Central BBQ: To kick off your Memphis adventure, head to Central BBQ at 147 E Butler Ave, Memphis, TN 38103. This local BBQ joint is renowned for its delicious smoked meats, and it's a perfect place to experience the city's culinary delights.

Afternoon

National Civil Rights Museum: Located at 450 Mulberry St, Memphis, TN 38103, this museum is situated in the former Lorraine Motel, where Dr. Martin Luther King Jr. was assassinated. It offers a compelling and educational experience for visitors of all ages.

Beale Street: After the museum, explore the historic Beale Street, known for its live music, vibrant atmosphere, and eclectic shops. It's a great place to experience the heart of Memphis culture.

Dinner

Huey's: Enjoy a family-friendly dinner at Huey's, a local burger joint famous for its unique atmosphere and delicious food. Visit the downtown location at 77 S 2nd St, Memphis, TN 38103.

Day 2: Fun and Learning

Morning

Memphis Zoo: Your family will have a blast at the Memphis Zoo, located at 2000 Prentiss Pl, Memphis, TN 38112. It's home to over 3,500 animals, including giant pandas, polar bears, and a giant sea lion.

Lunch

Tamp & Tap: Head to Tamp & Tap at 122 Gayoso Ave, Memphis, TN 38103, for a quick and tasty lunch. They offer a variety of sandwiches and coffee to refuel your energy.

Afternoon

Children's Museum of Memphis: The Children's Museum of Memphis, at 2525 Central Ave, Memphis, TN 38104, is a perfect place for kids to play and learn. It features interactive exhibits, an art studio, and a splash park.

Stax Museum of American Soul Music: Located at 926 E McLemore Ave, Memphis, TN 38106, this museum will introduce your family to the rich history of American soul music and its iconic artists.

Dinner

Gus's World Famous Fried Chicken: For a tasty dinner, try Gus's World Famous Fried Chicken at 310 S Front St, Memphis, TN 38103. Their spicy and crispy chicken is a local favorite.

Day 3: Music, History, and More

Morning

Graceland: You can't visit Memphis without experiencing the legacy of Elvis Presley. Graceland, at 3734 Elvis Presley Blvd, Memphis, TN 38116, is his former home and a fascinating museum.

Lunch

Marlowe's Ribs & Restaurant: Enjoy a classic Memphis meal at Marlowe's Ribs & Restaurant, located at 4381 Elvis Presley Blvd, Memphis, TN 38116. Their ribs and barbecue are a treat.

Afternoon

Mud Island River Park: Take your family to Mud Island River Park at 125 N Front St, Memphis, TN 38103. It offers a Riverwalk model, pedal boats, and an amphitheater.

Sun Studio: Discover the birthplace of rock 'n' roll at Sun Studio, located at 706 Union Ave, Memphis, TN 38103. This historic recording studio has hosted legends like Elvis Presley and Johnny Cash.

Dinner

Rendezvous BBQ: For a delectable barbecue dinner, try the Rendezvous BBQ at 52 S 2nd St, Memphis, TN 38103. Their charcoal-broiled ribs are a local specialty.

Day 4: Outdoor Adventures and Departure

Morning

Shelby Farms Greenline: Enjoy a peaceful morning bike ride or walk on the Shelby Farms Greenline, a 10.65-mile urban trail that starts at Tillman St and Barksdale St, Memphis, TN 38104.

Lunch

Gibson's Donuts: Treat your family to some delightful donuts from Gibson's Donuts at 760 Mount Moriah Rd, Memphis, TN 38117. It's a local favorite.

Afternoon

Memphis Botanic Garden: Conclude your trip with a visit to the Memphis Botanic Garden, located at 750 Cherry Rd, Memphis, TN 38117. It's a beautiful and tranquil place to relax before your departure.

Departure: Depending on your travel plans, head back to Memphis International Airport for your return flight.

Memphis offers an incredible array of family-friendly activities and attractions, making it the perfect destination for a memorable family vacation. This itinerary provides you with a well-rounded experience of the city's history, culture, music, and outdoor adventures. Enjoy your time in Memphis, and create lasting memories with your loved ones!

5-day travel Itinerary

Here's a comprehensive 5-day travel itinerary for visiting Memphis, complete with a variety of activities and their corresponding addresses to make the most of your trip to this vibrant city:

Day 1: Exploring Downtown Memphis

Morning:

Breakfast at The Arcade Restaurant
Address: 540 S Main St, Memphis, TN 38103
Start your day with a classic Southern breakfast at The Arcade Restaurant, one of Memphis' oldest restaurants.

Stroll along the Mississippi Riverfront
Head to Tom Lee Park for a relaxing walk along the Mississippi River. Enjoy scenic views and the historical significance of the riverfront.

Lunch:

Lunch at Gus's World Famous Fried Chicken
Address: 310 S Front St, Memphis, TN 38103

Savor the city's best fried chicken at Gus's. Their secret recipe and crispy, spicy chicken are legendary.
Afternoon:

Sun Studio Tour
Address: 706 Union Ave, Memphis, TN 38103
Discover the birthplace of rock 'n' roll with a tour of Sun Studio, where legendary artists like Elvis Presley and Johnny Cash recorded their music.

Stax Museum of American Soul Music
Address: 926 E McLemore Ave, Memphis, TN 38126
Explore the history of soul music and learn about iconic artists like Otis Redding at the Stax Museum.

Dinner:

Dinner at Rendezvous BBQ
Address: 52 S 2nd St, Memphis, TN 38103
Enjoy mouthwatering BBQ ribs and a unique atmosphere at the famous Rendezvous.

Day 2: Cultural Highlights and Food

Morning:

Graceland
Address: 3717 Elvis Presley Blvd, Memphis, TN 38116
Visit the home of Elvis Presley, the King of Rock and Roll, for a tour of Graceland Mansion and its exhibits.
Lunch:

Lunch at Central BBQ
Address: 147 E Butler Ave, Memphis, TN 38103
Indulge in more Memphis-style barbecue at Central BBQ, known for its delicious smoked meats and savory sauces.
Afternoon:

National Civil Rights Museum
Address: 450 Mulberry St, Memphis, TN 38103

Explore the history of the American Civil Rights Movement at the Lorraine Motel, where Dr. Martin Luther King Jr. was assassinated.

Memphis Zoo
Address: 2000 Prentiss Pl, Memphis, TN 38112
Spend the afternoon at the Memphis Zoo, home to a wide variety of animals from around the world.

Dinner:

Dinner at Itta Bena
Address: 145 Beale St, Memphis, TN 38103
Dine in style at Itta Bena, a restaurant with a rooftop view of Beale Street, offering Southern-inspired cuisine and live jazz music.

Day 3: Music and Museums

Morning:

Visit Memphis Rock 'n' Soul Museum
Address: 191 Beale St, Memphis, TN 38103
Explore the history of Memphis music at the Rock 'n' Soul Museum, located on Beale Street.

Explore Beale Street
Wander down Beale Street, famous for its live music venues, shops, and vibrant atmosphere.

Lunch:

Lunch at Blues City Cafe
Address: 138 Beale St, Memphis, TN 38103
Savor Southern comfort food and live music at Blues City Cafe on Beale Street.

Afternoon:

Stroll through Overton Park
Address: 1914 Poplar Ave, Memphis, TN 38104
Visit Overton Park, a beautiful green space featuring the Memphis Brooks Museum of Art and the Memphis College of Art.

Memphis Brooks Museum of Art
Address: 1934 Poplar Ave, Memphis, TN 38104
Explore a diverse collection of art, including American, European, and contemporary pieces.

Dinner:

Dinner at Flight Restaurant and Wine Bar
Address: 39 S Main St, Memphis, TN 38103
Enjoy a unique dining experience with a variety of small plates and wine pairings at Flight Restaurant.

Day 4: Day Trip to Mississippi

Morning:

Drive to Tunica, Mississippi
Take a day trip to the nearby town of Tunica, Mississippi, known for its casinos and entertainment.
Lunch:

Lunch at Blue and White Restaurant
Address: 1355 US-61, Tunica, MS 38676
Satisfy your Southern food cravings with a meal at the Blue and White Restaurant in Tunica.
Afternoon:

Horseshoe Tunica Casino
Address: 1021 Casino Center Dr, Robinsonville, MS 38664
Try your luck at Horseshoe Tunica Casino, featuring a variety of gaming options.

Tunica RiverPark & Museum
Address: 1 River Park Dr, Tunica, MS 38676
Learn about the history and culture of the Mississippi Delta at the RiverPark & Museum.

Dinner:

Dinner at Fitzgerald's Casino & Hotel
Address: 711 Lucky Ln, Robinsonville, MS 38664
Enjoy a delicious dinner at Fitzgerald's Casino & Hotel before returning to Memphis.

Day 5: Nature and Departure

Morning:

Shelby Farms Park
Address: 6903 Great View Dr N, Memphis, TN 38134
Spend your morning at Shelby Farms Park, one of the largest urban parks in the United States, offering hiking, biking, and picnicking opportunities.
Lunch:

Lunch at The Farmer
Address: 262 S Highland St, Memphis, TN 38111
Enjoy farm-to-table cuisine at The Farmer, known for its fresh and locally sourced ingredients.
Afternoon:

Memphis Botanic Garden
Address: 750 Cherry Rd, Memphis, TN 38117

Explore the beautiful Memphis Botanic Garden, featuring various themed gardens and a tranquil atmosphere.

Visit Grind City Brewing Company
Address: 76 Waterworks Ave, Memphis, TN 38107
Sample some of Memphis's finest craft beers at Grind City Brewing Company.

Evening:

Dinner at Flight Restaurant and Wine Bar (for a return visit)
Address: 39 S Main St, Memphis, TN 38103
End your trip with a delightful return to Flight Restaurant for a memorable final meal.

This 5-day itinerary provides a mix of history, culture, music, and culinary delights, allowing you to experience the best of Memphis. Make sure to book your accommodations in advance and adjust the schedule to your preferences and opening hours of attractions. Memphis is a city known for its rich history, soulful music, and delicious food, so be sure to savor every moment during your visit.

7-day Travel itinerary

here's a comprehensive 7-day travel itinerary for exploring Memphis, complete with various activities and their corresponding addresses. Memphis is a city known for its rich history, music, and delicious food, and this itinerary will help you make the most of your visit.

Day 1: Beale Street and Downtown Memphis

Morning:

Breakfast at The Arcade Restaurant
Address: 540 S Main St, Memphis, TN 38103

Start your day with a classic Southern breakfast at the oldest cafe in Memphis.

Late Morning:

Stroll along Beale Street
Address: Beale St, Memphis, TN 38103
Explore the iconic Beale Street, known for its vibrant music scene and historic significance.

Lunch:

Gus's World Famous Fried Chicken
Address: 310 S Front St, Memphis, TN 38103
Enjoy some of the best fried chicken in town.

Afternoon:

Visit the National Civil Rights Museum
Address: 450 Mulberry St, Memphis, TN 38103
Explore the history of the civil rights movement at this important museum.

Evening:

Dinner at Rendezvous BBQ
Address: 52 S 2nd St, Memphis, TN 38103
Savor Memphis-style barbecue at this legendary establishment.

Day 2: Graceland and Elvis Presley

Morning:

Graceland
Address: 3734 Elvis Presley Blvd, Memphis, TN 38116

Explore the former home of Elvis Presley, the King of Rock 'n' Roll.

Lunch:

Vernon's Smokehouse
Address: 3000 E Elvis Presley Blvd, Memphis, TN 38116
Enjoy a classic BBQ lunch near Graceland.

Afternoon:

Stax Museum of American Soul Music
Address: 926 E McLemore Ave, Memphis, TN 38126
Discover the history of American soul music and its legends.

Evening:

Sun Studio
Address: 706 Union Ave, Memphis, TN 38103
Visit the birthplace of rock 'n' roll and take a guided tour.

Day 3: Nature and Outdoors

Morning:

Shelby Farms Park
Address: 6903 Great View Dr N, Memphis, TN 38134
Enjoy the great outdoors with hiking, biking, and various activities.

Lunch:

Fuel Café
Address: 1761 N Watkins St, Memphis, TN 38107
Have a healthy and delicious lunch at this local favorite.

Afternoon:

Memphis Botanic Garden
Address: 750 Cherry Rd, Memphis, TN 38117
Stroll through beautiful gardens and relax in this serene setting.

Evening:

Dinner at The Second Line
Address: 2144 Monroe Ave, Memphis, TN 38104
Savor some of the best Creole and Southern cuisine in town.

Day 4: Museums and Art

Morning:

Memphis Brooks Museum of Art
Address: 1934 Poplar Ave, Memphis, TN 38104
Explore a diverse collection of art spanning centuries and cultures.

Lunch:

Babalu Tacos & Tapas
Address: 2115 Madison Ave, Memphis, TN 38104
Have a lunch of delicious tacos and tapas.

Afternoon:

Memphis Rock 'n' Soul Museum
Address: 191 Beale St, Memphis, TN 38103
Discover the birth of rock and soul music.

Evening:

Dinner at Flight
Address: 39 S Main St, Memphis, TN 38103
Experience a unique dining concept with small plates and wine flights.

Day 5: Mississippi River and Entertainment

Morning:

Mud Island River Park
Address: 125 N Front St, Memphis, TN 38103
Explore a river-themed park, and don't miss the Riverwalk Model.

Lunch:

Tug's Casual Grill
Address: 51 Harbor Town Square, Memphis, TN 38103
Enjoy a casual lunch with a view of the river.

Afternoon:

Memphis Riverboats
Address: 45 S Riverside Dr, Memphis, TN 38103
Take a riverboat cruise along the Mississippi River.

Evening:

Live Music on Beale Street
Address: Beale St, Memphis, TN 38103
Enjoy the live music and vibrant atmosphere in the heart of Memphis.

Day 6: Food and Local Flavors

Morning:

Soul Fish Café
Address: 862 S Cooper St, Memphis, TN 38104
Start your day with some delicious Southern-inspired breakfast.

Lunch:

Central BBQ
Address: 147 E Butler Ave, Memphis, TN 38103
Feast on some of the best BBQ in Memphis.

Afternoon:

Memphis Farmers Market (seasonal)
Address: 415 G.E. Patterson Ave, Memphis, TN 38103
Explore a variety of local produce, crafts, and artisanal foods.
Evening:

Gibson's Donuts
Address: 760 Mount Moriah Rd, Memphis, TN 38117
Enjoy a sweet treat from this popular local donut shop.

Day 7: History and Departure

Morning:

Slave Haven Underground Railroad Museum
Address: 826 N 2nd St, Memphis, TN 38107
Learn about Memphis's role in the Underground Railroad.

Lunch:

Gus's World Famous Fried Chicken (Downtown location)
Address: 310 S Front St, Memphis, TN 38103
A perfect last meal in Memphis.
Afternoon:

Sunset at Shelby Farms Park
Address: 6903 Great View Dr N, Memphis, TN 38134
Enjoy a relaxing afternoon and watch the sunset.

Evening:

Departure
Head to Memphis International Airport or your next destination, taking with you wonderful memories of your Memphis adventure.

This 7-day travel itinerary offers a well-rounded experience of Memphis, from its rich musical heritage to its delicious culinary scene and historical significance. Be sure to check the hours and availability of these attractions in advance and make any necessary reservations to ensure a smooth and memorable trip to the Home of the Blues and the Birthplace of Rock 'n' Roll.

Cultural Experiences

Festival and Events

Memphis, Tennessee is known for its lively music scene, delicious food, and a wide array of exciting festivals and events throughout the year. Whether you're a music enthusiast, a foodie, or just looking for a good time, Memphis has something to offer you. we'll explore some of the best festivals and events to check out when visiting Memphis, complete with their respective dates.

Beale Street Music Festival
Date: Early May

If you're a fan of live music, the Beale Street Music Festival is a must-visit event. This annual three-day music festival kicks off the Memphis in May International Festival and takes place in Tom Lee Park, right on the banks of the mighty Mississippi River. The lineup is always diverse, featuring an array of genres, including rock, blues, soul, and more. Past headliners have included legends like B.B. King, The Black Keys, and Post Malone.

Memphis in May International Festival
Date: Throughout May

Memphis in May is a month-long celebration of the city's heritage, culture, and international connections. The festival includes events like the World Championship Barbecue Cooking Contest, where you can sample some of the best barbecue in the world. There's also the Great American River Run, a marathon that takes you through the scenic streets of Memphis. The festival culminates with the Beale Street Music Festival, as mentioned earlier.

Memphis Food & Wine Festival
Date: October

For the culinary connoisseurs, the Memphis Food & Wine Festival is a highlight. It's a celebration of all things gastronomic, featuring dishes prepared by renowned chefs and exquisite wines from around the world. This event takes place in the Memphis Botanic Garden, creating a stunning backdrop for an unforgettable food and wine experience.

Memphis Italian Festival
Date: June

The Memphis Italian Festival celebrates the city's rich Italian heritage. This family-friendly event features live music, delicious Italian cuisine, a bocce ball tournament, and more. It's a great opportunity to savor authentic Italian food and immerse yourself in the local culture.

Memphis Music & Heritage Festival
Date: Labor Day Weekend

Labor Day Weekend is a fantastic time to be in Memphis, as it hosts the Memphis Music & Heritage Festival. This event showcases the city's diverse musical heritage, with live performances ranging from blues and gospel to rock 'n' roll and jazz. Stages are set up along Main Street, and you can enjoy an array of local talent.

Memphis Comedy Festival
Date: March

Laugh your heart out at the Memphis Comedy Festival, which features a lineup of stand-up comedians and improv groups from across the nation. The festival takes place in various venues throughout the city, and it's a great opportunity to enjoy some light-hearted entertainment.

Memphis International Jazz Festival
Date: November

Jazz lovers, rejoice! The Memphis International Jazz Festival brings world-class jazz performances to the city, paying homage to Memphis's deep-rooted connection to this genre of music. The festival hosts both local talents and international jazz musicians who put on unforgettable shows.

Memphis Brewfest
Date: April

If you're a craft beer enthusiast, the Memphis Brewfest is the perfect event for you. Sample a wide variety of local and regional craft beers in AutoZone Park, home to the Memphis Redbirds. This festival also features live music and food trucks, making it a delightful experience for beer and food lovers alike.

Memphis Film Festival
Date: April

For film buffs, the Memphis Film Festival is a must-attend event. It's an annual celebration of independent, classic, and international films. The festival screens a diverse selection of movies and hosts Q&A sessions with filmmakers and actors. It's a great opportunity to explore the world of cinema in a vibrant cultural setting.

Memphis Fashion Week
Date: Spring

Fashionistas will enjoy Memphis Fashion Week, a multi-day event that showcases local designers and emerging talents in the fashion industry. It includes runway shows, pop-up shops, and various fashion-related events, bringing a touch of glamour to the city.

Memphis Children's Theatre Festival
Date: April

If you're visiting Memphis with kids, the Memphis Children's Theatre Festival is a wonderful event to consider. It features performances specifically designed for young audiences, interactive workshops, and opportunities for children to engage with the world of theater.

Indie Memphis Film Festival
Date: October

Indie film enthusiasts shouldn't miss the Indie Memphis Film Festival. This event showcases independent films, highlighting the creativity and diversity of the filmmaking industry. It's a great platform for emerging filmmakers and a chance to discover unique and thought-provoking films.

From music and food to film and fashion, the city has something for everyone. When planning your trip to Memphis, be sure to check the dates of these events to make the most of your visit and immerse yourself in the vibrant atmosphere that this city has to offer. No matter when you visit, you'll find something exciting happening in Memphis to make your trip truly memorable.

Historical Sites and Museums

When visiting Memphis, you'll have the opportunity to explore a treasure trove of historical sites and museums that offer insights into the city's rich past and its significant contributions to music, civil rights, and more. In this guide, we'll take you on a tour of some of the best historical sites and museums in Memphis, complete with their addresses to help you plan your visit.

Graceland - Elvis Presley's Home
Address: 3734 Elvis Presley Blvd, Memphis, TN 38116
Graceland, the former home of the King of Rock 'n' Roll, Elvis Presley, is undoubtedly one of the most iconic attractions in Memphis. The mansion, known for its opulent interiors and the Meditation Garden where Elvis is buried, provides a unique glimpse into the life of the legendary musician. Tour the rooms, see his extensive car collection, and immerse yourself in the legacy of Elvis. It's an experience that shouldn't be missed.

National Civil Rights Museum
Address: 450 Mulberry St, Memphis, TN 38103
The National Civil Rights Museum is situated at the Lorraine Motel, where Dr. Martin Luther King Jr. was tragically assassinated in 1968. The museum is a poignant tribute to the civil rights movement and showcases the struggles and triumphs of African Americans. Visitors can explore exhibits that trace the journey from slavery to the civil rights era, including powerful displays on Rosa Parks, the Montgomery Bus Boycott, and Dr. King's legacy.

Stax Museum of American Soul Music
Address: 926 E McLemore Ave, Memphis, TN 38126
Stax Records played a pivotal role in the evolution of soul music, and the Stax Museum of American Soul Music offers a window into this influential genre. Visitors can discover the

history of artists like Otis Redding, Isaac Hayes, and Booker T. & the MGs, who recorded at Stax. Explore interactive exhibits, listen to soulful tunes, and see the original studio and instruments that produced some of the most beloved songs in American music history.

Sun Studio
Address: 706 Union Ave, Memphis, TN 38103
Known as the "Birthplace of Rock 'n' Roll," Sun Studio is where legendary musicians like Elvis Presley, Johnny Cash, and Jerry Lee Lewis launched their careers. Take a guided tour to witness the studio's vintage equipment and hear stories about the artists who recorded here. The tour will transport you back in time to the early days of rock music, making it an essential stop for any music lover.

Slave Haven Underground Railroad Museum
Address: 826 N 2nd St, Memphis, TN 38107
The Slave Haven Underground Railroad Museum, also known as the Burkle Estate, was a stop on the Underground Railroad during the 19th century. It offers a fascinating glimpse into the lives of enslaved individuals who sought freedom on their journey to the north. Explore the hidden passages and secret chambers used to shelter escaping slaves, and learn about the daring individuals who provided refuge.

Cotton Museum
Address: 65 Union Ave, Memphis, TN 38103
Cotton has played a vital role in the history of Memphis, and the Cotton Museum offers a captivating narrative of the cotton industry's influence on the city and the South as a whole. Through multimedia exhibits, visitors can understand the economic, social, and cultural impact of cotton and the people who labored in the fields.

Memphis Rock 'n' Soul Museum
Address: 191 Beale St, Memphis, TN 38103
Located on Beale Street, the Memphis Rock 'n' Soul Museum explores the birth of rock and soul music. This Smithsonian-affiliated museum delves into the cultural and social changes that paved the way for these revolutionary genres. Interactive exhibits and artifacts from the likes of B.B. King and Elvis Presley illustrate the evolution of music in Memphis.

Elmwood Cemetery
Address: 824 S Dudley St, Memphis, TN 38104
Elmwood Cemetery is not only a burial place but also a remarkable historical site in Memphis. The cemetery, dating back to 1852, houses the graves of prominent figures from the city's past. Take a guided tour to learn about the people buried here, their stories, and the beautifully landscaped grounds.

Memphis Brooks Museum of Art
Address: 1934 Poplar Ave, Memphis, TN 38104
The Memphis Brooks Museum of Art is the oldest and largest art museum in Tennessee, featuring an impressive collection of art spanning various periods and styles. The museum is renowned for its European and American art, as well as its special exhibitions. It's a haven for art lovers and culture seekers.

Slave Haven Burkle Estate Museum
Address: 826 N 2nd St, Memphis, TN 38107

The Slave Haven Burkle Estate Museum, formerly the Burkle Estate, offers a powerful and educational experience for those interested in the history of the Underground Railroad and the struggles of enslaved people in the South. This historic home served as a refuge for freedom seekers and provides a unique perspective on the challenges faced during this tumultuous time in American history.

Pink Palace Museum
Address: 3050 Central Ave, Memphis, TN 38111

The Pink Palace Museum is a Memphis institution that explores a wide range of topics, from the history of the Mid-South to the mysteries of outer space. The museum is housed in a beautiful pink Georgian-style mansion and offers exhibits on local culture, natural history, and the universe. One of the highlights is the CTI 3D Giant Theater, where you can enjoy educational and entertaining films.

Mississippi River Park
Address: Riverside Dr, Memphis, TN 38103

The Mississippi River is integral to the history and culture of Memphis, and the Mississippi River Park allows you to take in the beauty and significance of this mighty waterway. The park features walking trails, picnic areas, and stunning views of the river. It's a peaceful place to reflect on the historical importance of the Mississippi in the city's development.

Memphis, Tennessee, is a city steeped in history, from the birth of rock 'n' roll to its pivotal role in the civil rights movement. These historical sites and museums offer a rich tapestry of experiences, providing valuable insights into the city's past and its contributions to American culture. Whether you're a music aficionado, a history buff, or simply a curious traveler, Memphis has something to offer for everyone seeking to explore its fascinating history and heritage. Be sure to plan your visit to these sites, each with its own unique story to tell and address to help you find your way.

Culture & Etiquette

When you're planning a visit to Memphis, Tennessee, it's essential to understand and appreciate the local culture and etiquette. Memphis is a city known for its rich musical heritage, soulful food, and a strong sense of community. To ensure you have a memorable and respectful visit, here's a guide to the culture and etiquette you should be aware of:

1. Music is the Heartbeat:

Memphis is often hailed as the "Home of the Blues" and the "Birthplace of Rock 'n' Roll." It's where legends like Elvis Presley, B.B. King, and Johnny Cash left their mark. Memphis residents take immense pride in their music heritage, so make sure to immerse yourself in the local music scene. Be respectful when visiting iconic places like Graceland, Sun Studio, or Stax Museum of American Soul Music. Embrace the rhythm of Beale Street, and remember that music is a way of life here.

2. Southern Hospitality:

Southern hospitality is more than just a phrase; it's a way of life in Memphis. Expect to be greeted with warmth and friendliness wherever you go. It's customary to say "please" and "thank you" and to engage in small talk. People often hold doors for each other and offer assistance when needed. Return the kindness with a smile and a friendly attitude.

3. Dress Respectfully:

When in Memphis, dress modestly and comfortably. While the city is known for its music and nightlife, it's important to respect local traditions. In some churches and more formal establishments, you might be expected to dress up a bit.

However, casual attire is generally acceptable in most places, especially during the warmer months.

4. Food Culture:

Memphis is famous for its barbecue, and there are numerous places to savor this southern delicacy. When enjoying local cuisine, remember that it's acceptable to use your hands when eating ribs or fried chicken. It's all part of the experience. However, do ask for extra napkins; it can get messy. Also, it's customary to tip your server, and a 15-20% tip is appreciated.

5. Respect the Church:

Memphis has a strong religious community, and many residents are deeply religious. If you plan to visit a church or attend a religious event, dress modestly and be on your best behavior. It's a sign of respect to be quiet and attentive during religious services.

6. Festivals and Events:

Memphis hosts numerous festivals and events throughout the year, such as the Beale Street Music Festival, Memphis in May, and the Memphis International Jazz Festival. These events are a great way to experience the local culture and enjoy some live music. Be respectful of others, follow the event rules, and make the most of these fantastic gatherings.

7. Memphis Grizzlies and University of Memphis Tigers:

If you're a sports fan, you may want to catch a game of basketball. The Memphis Grizzlies and the University of Memphis Tigers both have passionate fan bases. If attending a game, support the local team, and enjoy the camaraderie that comes with cheering alongside Memphians.

8. Traffic Etiquette:

Memphis, like any other city, has its share of traffic. Be patient, follow the local traffic laws, and drive courteously. Memphis drivers tend to be considerate and will often let you merge or change lanes, so return the favor with a friendly wave or nod.

9. Learn the Local Lingo:

Memphis has its own unique slang and phrases. For example, "y'all" is a common contraction of "you all," and "bless your heart" can be both a term of sympathy and a passive-aggressive phrase. Don't be afraid to ask locals about these phrases; they'll likely appreciate your interest.

10. Safety First:

While Memphis is a vibrant city, it's essential to stay aware of your surroundings and take necessary safety precautions. Like in any urban area, be cautious in unfamiliar neighborhoods, avoid walking alone at night in less well-lit areas, and lock your car and accommodations.

11. Graceland Respect:

Graceland, the former home of Elvis Presley, is a major attraction in Memphis. When visiting, be respectful of the place and the people who consider it a shrine. Avoid making jokes or disrespectful comments, and follow the rules and guidelines provided by the staff.

12. Tipping Etiquette:

Tipping is a customary practice in Memphis, as it is in the rest of the United States. It's customary to tip at restaurants, bars, and for services like taxis or rideshares. The standard tip is 15-20% of the total bill.

13. Mind the Delta Blues:

The Mississippi Delta is a significant part of Memphis's cultural heritage. It's where the blues genre was born. When visiting this region, be sure to pay homage to its rich history. The Delta Blues Museum in nearby Clarksdale, Mississippi, is a great place to start.

14. Be Mindful of Events and History:

Memphis played a pivotal role in the Civil Rights Movement, with the National Civil Rights Museum located at the Lorraine Motel, where Dr. Martin Luther King Jr. was assassinated. When visiting this important site, show respect and learn about this crucial chapter in American history.

15. Enjoy the Food Scene:

Memphis is renowned for its diverse food scene. In addition to barbecue, you'll find a variety of southern dishes, including catfish, hot tamales, and soul food. Explore different cuisines and be open to trying new flavors.

16. Family Values:

Family is highly valued in Memphis. If you're invited to someone's home, bring a small gift or dessert to share. Engage in conversations about family, as it's a common and cherished topic among locals.

17. Nightlife Etiquette:

Memphis offers a vibrant nightlife with bars, clubs, and live music venues. When enjoying the nightlife, be respectful of other patrons, follow the venue's rules, and drink responsibly. Also, remember that smoking may not be allowed in certain establishments, so be mindful of designated smoking areas.

18. Gratitude and Thankfulness:

Expressing gratitude is a significant part of the local culture. Whether it's for a meal, a kind gesture, or someone holding a door for you, saying "thank you" goes a long way in Memphis. This simple act of appreciation is an integral part of the city's charm.

Understanding and respecting the local culture and etiquette will not only enhance your experience but also show your appreciation for this incredible city. Embrace the music, savor the food, and engage with the people of Memphis to truly immerse yourself in its vibrant and rich cultural tapestry. Enjoy your visit to the "Home of the Blues" and the heart of southern hospitality.

Off the Beaten Path Adventures

Hidden Gems & lesser known Destinations to check out

While famous for its iconic Beale Street and Graceland, there is a treasure trove of hidden gems and lesser-known destinations that await the curious traveler. If you're planning a trip to Memphis and want to explore beyond the well-trodden path, here are some unique places to add to your itinerary.

Stax Museum of American Soul Music

Location: 926 East McLemore Ave, Memphis, TN 38126
The Stax Museum is a mecca for soul music lovers and history buffs alike. This unassuming building houses an extraordinary collection of artifacts and memorabilia from the Stax Records era, a label that produced some of the most iconic soul music in history. As you explore, you'll find instruments played by legends like Otis Redding and Booker T. & the MG's, as well as original clothing worn by artists.

But the museum is more than just a place to view items behind glass. It immerses you in the history of the time, particularly the Civil Rights Movement. Displays vividly depict the socio-political backdrop against which this soulful music emerged. You can even stand on the original stage from the Stax recording studio and feel the echoes of soul legends.

Memphis Zoo

Location: 2000 Prentiss Pl, Memphis, TN 38112
While the Memphis Zoo may not be a hidden gem, it's often overshadowed by the city's other attractions. With over 3,500 animals from more than 500 species, this sprawling 70-acre zoo is a hidden treasure for wildlife enthusiasts. The African Savannah exhibit, with its giraffes and zebras, feels like a safari adventure.

One of the highlights is the Teton Trek, which transports you to the wilds of Yellowstone. Grizzly bears, wolves, and elk are among the stars of this immersive exhibit. Additionally, the Giant Panda exhibit, featuring the charming pandas Ya Ya and Le Le, is a unique experience. Educational programs and animal encounters are regular features, making the Memphis Zoo an excellent destination for learning and family fun.

Victorian Village

Location: Adams Ave, Memphis, TN 38103
The Victorian Village is a step back in time to the opulence of the late 19th century. Strolling along Adams Avenue, you'll encounter an array of historic mansions, some of which have been transformed into museums open to the public.

The Mallory-Neely House is one such mansion. A guided tour takes you through this ornate home, showcasing period furniture, clothing, and the stories of the families who lived there. It's a captivating look at the lifestyle of Memphis's elite during the Gilded Age.

Slave Haven Underground Railroad Museum

Location: 826 N 2nd St, Memphis, TN 38107

The Slave Haven Underground Railroad Museum, also known as the Burkle Estate, provides a unique and immersive experience. This historic house was a stop on the Underground Railroad, a secret network of safehouses that helped enslaved people escape to freedom.

Guided tours allow you to explore hidden passageways, trapdoors, and secret rooms used to shelter those seeking freedom. The museum displays artifacts and exhibits that offer a profound look into the daring escapes and the brave individuals who risked everything to help enslaved people escape to freedom.

Mud Island River Park

Location: 125 N Front St, Memphis, TN 38103
Mud Island River Park is a serene oasis nestled along the Mississippi River. One of its unique features is the Riverwalk model, a scale replica of the Mississippi River. As you walk along this model, you can appreciate the geography, history, and culture of the communities that line the river.

The park also houses an amphitheater where you can catch live performances, from concerts to outdoor movies. If you're up for some physical activity, consider renting a pedal boat and cruising around the park's scenic pond. The park's River Terrace offers a fantastic view of the Mississippi River and the Memphis skyline.

Cotton Museum

Location: 65 Union Ave, Memphis, TN 38103
Memphis's history is intrinsically linked to the cotton industry, and the Cotton Museum does an exceptional job of showcasing this history. Located in the historic Memphis Cotton Exchange Building, the museum tells the story of

cotton, from its role in the economy to its impact on the social fabric of the region.

You can explore exhibits that detail the cotton trade, view cotton-related artifacts, and learn about the labor-intensive process of cotton production. It's a comprehensive and eye-opening look at the industry that once dominated the city.

Chucalissa Archaeological Museum

Location: 1987 Indian Village Dr, Memphis, TN 38109
Situated within the grounds of T.O. Fuller State Park, the Chucalissa Archaeological Museum focuses on the Native American history of the Mississippi Delta region. The museum features both indoor exhibits and an outdoor archaeological site.

The outdoor site allows visitors to step back in time, where they can explore the remains of a 15th-century Native American village. The museum's exhibits offer insights into the lives of the indigenous peoples who once inhabited the area. It's an opportunity to connect with the deep-rooted history of the region.

National Ornamental Metal Museum

Location: 374 Metal Museum Dr, Memphis, TN 38106
Overlooking the Mississippi River, the National Ornamental Metal Museum is a hidden treasure for art enthusiasts. The museum celebrates the art of metalworking, showcasing intricate sculptures, functional art pieces, and ornamental works.

One of the unique aspects of the museum is the working blacksmith shop, where you can witness the craft in action. The museum regularly hosts rotating exhibitions that feature the creative work of metal artists from around the world. The serene riverside location provides a beautiful backdrop for appreciating the craftsmanship on display.

A. Schwab Trading Co.

Location: 163 Beale St, Memphis, TN 38103
A. Schwab Trading Co. is more than just a store; it's a time machine that takes you back to the late 19th century. The store has been a part of Memphis's history since 1876 and is a cherished piece of the city's heritage.

As you wander through its aisles, you'll discover a wide array of goods, from old-fashioned remedies and quirky novelties to vintage-style candy and unique souvenirs. It's a nostalgic and delightful shopping experience, and you'll find items here that you won't see in modern stores.

Memphis Farmers Market

Location: 409 S Main St, Memphis, TN 38103
The Memphis Farmers Market is a hub for culinary enthusiasts and lovers of fresh, locally sourced produce. Open every Saturday, it's a vibrant and dynamic marketplace where local farmers, artisans, and food vendors come together.

Explore a colorful array of fruits, vegetables, meats, cheeses, and artisanal products. Food trucks offer a variety of culinary delights, and you can engage in conversations with the farmers and producers, gaining insight into the region's rich agricultural scene.

Location: 5992 Quince Rd, Memphis, TN 38119

The Lichterman Nature Center is a tranquil haven within the city of Memphis. This 65-acre urban nature preserve is dedicated to environmental education and the appreciation of the natural world. The center's pristine trails wind through diverse ecosystems, including hardwood forests, meadows, and a lake.

As you explore the trails, you'll have the opportunity to observe local wildlife, including various species of birds, reptiles, and amphibians. The lake is a serene spot for birdwatching and picnicking, and the educational exhibits within the visitor center provide valuable insights into the region's natural history.

Minglewood Hall

Location: 1555 Madison Ave, Memphis, TN 38104
Minglewood Hall is a lesser-known but vibrant music and entertainment venue. Located in the vibrant Cooper-Young district, the venue offers a platform for a wide range of performances, from local indie bands to nationally recognized artists.

The hall's schedule is diverse, featuring live music concerts, comedy shows, and other forms of entertainment. It's an intimate space that allows you to get up close and personal with the performers, making for a memorable and unique experience.

Mississippi Greenbelt Park

Location: Along the Mississippi River, Memphis, TN 38103
Memphis's Mississippi Greenbelt Park is a hidden gem for nature lovers and outdoor enthusiasts. This park stretches along the banks of the mighty Mississippi River and offers an

opportunity to escape the urban bustle and immerse yourself in the region's natural beauty.

The park's trails wind through lush woodlands, providing a peaceful environment for hiking, birdwatching, and picnicking. Cyclists can enjoy leisurely rides along the river, taking in the scenic views of the Mississippi. The park is an ideal location to connect with the natural world and unwind in a serene setting.

Cooper-Young Historic District

Location: Cooper St & Young Ave, Memphis, TN 38104
The Cooper-Young Historic District is a trendy and vibrant neighborhood that's often overlooked by tourists in favor of more famous areas like Beale Street. This district is a hotspot for the local community and boasts a thriving arts and culinary scene.

As you explore the district, you'll discover an eclectic mix of boutiques, coffee shops, vintage stores, art galleries, and restaurants. The streets are adorned with vibrant street art and murals, adding to the district's unique character. It's an excellent place to soak in the local culture, enjoy delicious cuisine, and find distinctive souvenirs.

Metal Arts Meetup

Location: Various locations, check their website for details
The Metal Arts Meetup is a fantastic resource for anyone interested in metalworking, jewelry making, and blacksmithing. This community-driven group offers workshops and gatherings at various locations around Memphis, making it a great opportunity to connect with local artisans and learn about the art of metal.

Workshops cover a wide range of topics, from basic metalworking techniques to advanced artistic projects. It's a chance to get hands-on experience and gain insights into the creative world of metal artistry. Be sure to check their website for upcoming events and locations.

In conclusion, these hidden gems and lesser-known destinations in Memphis provide a diverse array of experiences, from deep dives into the city's musical history and architectural beauty to explorations of its significant historical sites and the serene embrace of its natural settings. By venturing off the beaten path and discovering these hidden treasures, you'll gain a profound appreciation for Memphis's multifaceted identity and create lasting memories that go beyond the typical tourist experience. Whether you're a history enthusiast, nature lover, or a music aficionado, Memphis has something special to offer.

Fun things to do during your visit

We'll explore some of the best fun things to do during your visit to Memphis, ensuring you have a memorable and enjoyable experience in this vibrant city.

1. Graceland: Pay Tribute to the King

Your visit to Memphis would not be complete without a trip to Graceland, the iconic former home of Elvis Presley, the King of Rock 'n' Roll. Graceland is a place of pilgrimage for music enthusiasts, and it offers a unique opportunity to step back in time and explore the life of one of the most legendary figures in music history. Tour the mansion, view the exhibits, and see Elvis's car collection and custom planes.

2. Beale Street: Experience the Music Scene

Beale Street is often referred to as the "Home of the Blues." This historic street is a lively, vibrant hub of music, entertainment, and culture. With numerous clubs, bars, and restaurants, Beale Street offers a rich musical scene, with live performances happening almost every night. Enjoy some authentic Memphis blues and immerse yourself in the city's music culture.

3. Sun Studio: Where Rock 'n' Roll Was Born

Sun Studio is often called the "Birthplace of Rock 'n' Roll" and is a must-visit for music history enthusiasts. Here, you can take a guided tour and learn about the legendary musicians who recorded at this studio, including Elvis Presley, Johnny Cash, and Jerry Lee Lewis. The studio offers a fascinating journey through the history of American music.

4. Stax Museum of American Soul Music: Soulful Experience

Stax Museum is another fantastic attraction for music lovers, particularly fans of soul music. The museum is located at the original site of Stax Records, and it features a vast collection of memorabilia, exhibits, and artifacts related to the history of soul music and the artists who made it famous.

5. National Civil Rights Museum: A Lesson in History

Memphis played a pivotal role in the American Civil Rights Movement, and the National Civil Rights Museum is a powerful testament to that history. Housed in the former Lorraine Motel, where Dr. Martin Luther King Jr. was assassinated, this museum offers a comprehensive look at the struggle for civil rights in America. It's a moving and educational experience that's both sobering and inspiring.

6. Memphis Zoo: Fun for All Ages

For a family-friendly adventure, visit the Memphis Zoo. The zoo features a wide variety of animals from around the world, and it's a great place to spend the day with kids. From giant pandas to hippos and giraffes, the Memphis Zoo has a diverse collection of animals to admire.

7. Shelby Farms Park: Outdoor Fun

Shelby Farms Park is one of the largest urban parks in the United States, and it's an excellent spot for outdoor activities. You can go hiking, biking, or simply enjoy a picnic in this beautiful green space. The park also offers kayaking and paddleboarding on its lakes. If you're an outdoor enthusiast, this is the place for you.

8. Memphis Botanic Garden: Natural Beauty

For a more serene experience, visit the Memphis Botanic Garden. This 96-acre garden is a haven of tranquility with a wide variety of plants, flowers, and landscapes to admire. It's a perfect spot for a leisurely stroll or a picnic amidst the beauty of nature.

9. Mississippi River Park: Riverside Relaxation

The Mississippi River Park provides an opportunity to take in the scenic beauty of the mighty Mississippi River. You can walk or bike along the riverfront, have a picnic, or simply relax and enjoy the views. It's a peaceful escape from the hustle and bustle of the city.

10. Food and Dining: Savor Memphis's Culinary Delights

Memphis is known for its delectable food scene, particularly its barbecue. Don't leave without trying some authentic

Memphis-style barbecue at renowned spots like Gus's World Famous Fried Chicken, Central BBQ, or the Rendezvous. Beyond barbecue, you can also sample the city's diverse culinary offerings, including soul food, hot tamales, and more.

11. Overton Park: Cultural Hub

Overton Park is not just a green space but a cultural hub as well. It houses several attractions within its boundaries, including the Memphis Brooks Museum of Art and the Memphis College of Art. You can explore art and culture while enjoying the park's natural beauty.

12. Memphis Riverboats: Cruise the Mighty Mississippi

For a unique experience, consider taking a cruise on one of the Memphis Riverboats. You can enjoy dinner cruises, sightseeing tours, and even special event cruises while taking in the breathtaking views of the Mississippi River.

13. AutoZone Park: Baseball Enthusiasts

If you're a baseball fan, catch a game at AutoZone Park, home to the Memphis Redbirds, the Triple-A affiliate of the St. Louis Cardinals. The stadium offers a fun, family-friendly atmosphere to enjoy America's favorite pastime.

14. Memphis in May International Festival: Celebrate Culture

If your visit coincides with May, don't miss the Memphis in May International Festival. It's a month-long celebration of culture, music, and food, featuring events like the Beale Street Music Festival, the World Championship Barbecue Cooking Contest, and the Sunset Symphony. It's a vibrant and festive time to experience the city.

15. Memphis Rock 'n' Soul Museum: Dive into Music History

The Memphis Rock 'n' Soul Museum is a Smithsonian-affiliated museum that tells the story of the birth of rock and soul music. Interactive exhibits and artifacts provide a deeper understanding of the cultural and social changes that gave rise to these iconic music genres.

16. Memphis Music Hall of Fame: Honoring Legends

This museum is dedicated to honoring the legends of Memphis music. It's a great place to learn about the musicians and producers who have shaped the city's musical heritage.

17. Elmwood Cemetery: Historical Visit

Elmwood Cemetery is a historic cemetery that provides a fascinating glimpse into Memphis's past. It's the final resting place for many notable individuals, and you can take guided tours to learn about the city's history through its gravesites.

18. Memphis Escape Rooms: Test Your Wits

If you enjoy puzzles and challenges, try one of Memphis's escape rooms. These interactive games are perfect for groups looking for a fun and mentally stimulating experience.

19. Memphis Pyramid: Bass Pro Shops and More

The Memphis Pyramid is a massive retail and entertainment complex located within a transformed sports arena. Inside, you'll find a massive Bass Pro Shops store, an indoor swamp, an observation deck with stunning views of the Mississippi River, and even a bowling alley and hotel.

20. Ghost Tours: Spooky Adventures

If you're into the supernatural, take one of Memphis's ghost tours. These tours explore the city's haunted history and are a great way to learn about local legends and spooky stories.

21. Memphis Grizzlies Game: NBA Action

If you're a basketball fan, catch a Memphis Grizzlies game at the FedExForum. Watching an NBA game live can be an exciting and memorable experience.

22. Memphis River Parks: Scenic Beauty

Memphis has several parks along the riverfront, offering stunning views and a serene atmosphere. Take a leisurely walk, have a picnic, or simply enjoy the natural beauty of the Mississippi River.

23. Memphis Farmers' Market: Local Flavors

If you happen to visit Memphis on a weekend, check out the Memphis Farmers' Market. It's a great place to experience local flavors, purchase fresh produce, and explore unique arts and crafts.

24. South Main Arts District: Art and Shopping

South Main Arts District is a vibrant neighborhood with art galleries, boutiques, and restaurants. It's an excellent place for shopping, enjoying art, and exploring the local culture.

25. Mississippi River Pedestrian Park: Stroll by the River

For a relaxing riverside walk, visit the Mississippi River Pedestrian Park. It's a beautiful place to take a leisurely stroll, enjoy the breeze, and watch the riverboats pass by.

26. Cooper-Young Historic District: Bohemian Vibes

Cooper-Young is a trendy historic district with a bohemian feel. It's filled with eclectic shops, local eateries, and a vibrant atmosphere. Explore the unique boutiques and enjoy the laid-back vibes.

27. Slave Haven Underground Railroad Museum: Hidden History

Learn about the history of the Underground Railroad and the courageous people who helped enslaved individuals escape to freedom. This museum, located in a historic house, offers a glimpse into this important chapter of American history.

28. Shop at Memphis's Unique Boutiques

Memphis is known for its unique shopping scene. From vintage stores to artisan boutiques, there's a wide array of shops to explore and find one-of-a-kind items.

29. Memphis Breweries: Craft Beer Lovers

If you're a fan of craft beer, Memphis has a growing brewery scene. Visit some of the local breweries to sample their offerings and get a taste of Memphis's craft beer culture.

30. Cotton Museum: Explore the Cotton Industry

The Cotton Museum is a fascinating attraction that delves into the history of cotton and its significant impact on

Memphis and the South. It's a lesser-known gem that provides insight into the region's history and economy.

31. Memphis' Mural Art: Street Art Delights

Explore the city's vibrant mural art scene. Memphis is home to numerous stunning street art installations that reflect the city's culture and history.

32. Southland Casino Racing: Gaming and Entertainment

For those who enjoy gaming and horse racing, Southland Casino Racing offers a fun night out. It has a wide variety of slot machines, live racing, and dining options.

33. Memphis Flyer: Local Events

Before your visit, check out the Memphis Flyer, the city's alternative news source, for information on local events, concerts, and festivals happening during your stay.

34. Victorian Village: Historic Architecture

Take a stroll through Victorian Village to admire the grand Victorian-era homes and experience the architectural charm of Memphis.

35. Memphis Symphony Orchestra: Classical Music Lovers

If you appreciate classical music, consider attending a performance by the Memphis Symphony Orchestra. They offer a range of concerts throughout the year.

36. Visit the Birthplace of Aretha Franklin

Aretha Franklin, the Queen of Soul, was born in Memphis. Her childhood home is now a museum dedicated to her life and music, offering a unique glimpse into her early years.

37. T.O. Fuller State Park: Outdoor Adventures

For a day of outdoor fun, head to T.O. Fuller State Park. It features hiking trails, a golf course, and a swimming pool, providing various recreational opportunities.

38. National Ornamental Metal Museum: Artistic Metalwork

Explore the world of artistic metalwork at the National Ornamental Metal Museum. It showcases beautiful pieces of metal art and offers demonstrations of blacksmithing and metalworking techniques.

39. Memphis Shades and Street Art Tours: Artistic Exploration

Join a guided tour to explore Memphis's vibrant street art scene. These tours provide insight into the artists and inspirations behind the city's murals and graffiti.

40. Discover Hidden Gems in the Cooper-Young Historic District

Cooper-Young is known for its eclectic shops, but it's also a treasure trove of hidden gems. Explore the district to find unique vintage shops, art galleries, and delightful cafes.

41. Memphis Food Tours: Culinary Adventures

For a deeper dive into Memphis's food culture, consider taking a guided food tour. These tours lead you through the city's culinary hotspots, allowing you to sample a variety of dishes and learn about the city's food history.

42. Explore Memphis's Craft Cocktail Scene

Memphis has a growing craft cocktail scene. Visit local bars and lounges known for their innovative and creative drink menus. Try a Memphis-inspired cocktail and savor the city's unique flavors.

43. Explore Memphis's Cultural Festivals

Throughout the year, Memphis hosts a variety of cultural festivals celebrating different aspects of the city's culture. Whether it's the Memphis Italian Festival, Memphis Greek Festival, or Memphis in May, you can experience the rich diversity of the city's cultural heritage.

44. Memphis Farmers' Markets: Fresh and Local

In addition to the Memphis Farmers' Market, there are several other local markets in the area. These markets offer fresh produce, handmade goods, and an opportunity to engage with the local community.

45. Memphis Waterfront Walking Trails: Scenic Strolls

Memphis's riverfront offers scenic walking trails, making it a perfect spot for a leisurely stroll with beautiful views of the Mississippi River. The Riverwalk, Mississippi River Park, and the Big River Crossing are great options for taking in the scenery.

46. Memphis College of Art Gallery: Artistic Inspiration

The Memphis College of Art Gallery is a place to explore contemporary art created by both students and faculty. It's a wonderful opportunity to immerse yourself in the local art scene.

47. Visit Local Bookstores: Literary Delights

Memphis boasts a number of independent bookstores. Explore these unique shops to discover hidden literary treasures and support local businesses.

48. Learn About Memphis's African-American History

Memphis has a rich African-American history, and there are museums, historic sites, and guided tours that provide insight into the city's African-American heritage.

49. Explore the Mississippi River by Kayak

For a unique perspective of the Mississippi River, rent a kayak and paddle along its scenic shores. It's an adventurous and picturesque way to experience the river up close.

50. Memphis Metal Museum: Art and Craftsmanship

The Memphis Metal Museum is a unique institution dedicated to the art of fine metalwork. It features a collection of metal sculptures and offers educational programs and workshops for those interested in the craft.

51. Learn About the Cotton Industry at the Cotton Museum

The Cotton Museum provides an in-depth look into the history of cotton in Memphis and the South. It's an eye-opening experience that highlights the significance of cotton in shaping the city's economy and culture.

52. Memphis Urban Exploration: Abandoned Sites

For the adventurous and curious, there are urban exploration opportunities in Memphis. Explore abandoned sites, industrial ruins, and decaying buildings to uncover hidden stories of the city's past.

Outdoor Activities & Nature

Best Parks & Gardens in The City

what many visitors may not be aware of is the city's abundance of stunning parks and gardens that offer a peaceful escape from the bustling urban environment. Whether you're a nature enthusiast, a history buff, or simply seeking a tranquil place to relax, Memphis has a wide range of green spaces to explore. In this guide, we will highlight some of the best parks and gardens in Memphis, complete with their addresses to help you plan your visit.

Shelby Farms Park

Address: 6903 Great View Drive North, Memphis, TN 38134

Shelby Farms Park is a sprawling urban park that spans over 4,500 acres, making it one of the largest urban parks in the United States. The park offers a diverse range of activities, from hiking and biking trails to picnicking spots and playgrounds for children. There's also a picturesque lake where you can rent paddle boats, and even a herd of resident bison. One of the park's main attractions is the Shelby Farms Greenline, a 10.65-mile-long urban trail that connects the park to the heart of Memphis, offering a fantastic opportunity to explore the city's natural beauty.

Memphis Botanic Garden

Address: 750 Cherry Road, Memphis, TN 38117

If you're a fan of horticulture and love to immerse yourself in beautiful, well-maintained gardens, the Memphis Botanic Garden is a must-visit. Spread across 96 acres, this garden features a wide variety of themed gardens, including

Japanese, rose, and wildflower gardens. The My Big Backyard is a fantastic place for kids, and the Butterfly Garden is a favorite among visitors of all ages. The Memphis Botanic Garden hosts special events, plant sales, and educational programs throughout the year.

Overton Park

Address: 1914 Poplar Ave, Memphis, TN 38104

Overton Park is often considered the heart of Memphis and offers a mix of history, culture, and greenery. The park houses the Memphis Brooks Museum of Art and the Memphis College of Art. The centerpiece of Overton Park is the Memphis Zoo, a popular attraction for families. The Old Forest State Natural Area, located within the park, is a rare urban old-growth forest that provides a glimpse of the area's original landscape.

Tom Lee Park

Address: Riverside Drive, Memphis, TN 38103

Situated along the mighty Mississippi River, Tom Lee Park offers breathtaking views of the river, as well as ample green space for picnics, frisbee, and relaxation. Named after Tom Lee, a local hero who saved 32 people from a sinking steamboat in 1925, the park features a statue in his honor. The park is also the site of numerous festivals and events throughout the year, including the Memphis in May International Festival.

T.O. Fuller State Park

Address: 1500 Mitchell Rd, Memphis, TN 38109

T.O. Fuller State Park is an excellent place to experience the natural beauty of Tennessee. This state park covers over 1,138 acres and is known for its lush woodlands, pristine lakes, and a golf course. It's a great destination for outdoor activities like hiking, fishing, and birdwatching. The park also offers cabins and campgrounds, making it an ideal spot for those who want to spend a night in nature.

Dixon Gallery and Gardens

Address: 4339 Park Ave, Memphis, TN 38117

The Dixon Gallery and Gardens combines art and nature in a harmonious way. This museum features a remarkable collection of French Impressionist paintings and decorative arts, housed in a stunning neoclassical mansion. Outside, you'll find beautifully landscaped gardens, including terraces, fountains, and a woodland setting. The Dixon's gardens are particularly famous for their seasonal displays of daffodils, tulips, and camellias.

Hickory Hill Park

Address: 3910 Ridgeway Rd, Memphis, TN 38115

Hickory Hill Park is a well-kept secret in Memphis. This serene park features a peaceful lake surrounded by walking trails, making it an ideal spot for a leisurely stroll or a peaceful afternoon picnic. The park also has a playground for kids, making it a family-friendly destination. It's a place where you can unwind and connect with nature away from the city's hustle and bustle.

Audubon Park

Address: 751 Cherry Rd, Memphis, TN 38117

Audubon Park is a charming, 373-acre park nestled in the East Memphis area. This park offers a picturesque lake, walking paths, and ample space for picnics and relaxation. It's a popular spot for dog walkers and families, and its historic setting provides a sense of tranquility that's perfect for escaping the city's noise.

Martyr's Park

Address: 67 Riverside Dr, Memphis, TN 38103

Martyr's Park is a small but significant riverside park with a touching history. It's named in honor of those who died in the 1878 Yellow Fever epidemic. The park provides a quiet place to reflect, with stunning views of the Mississippi River and the Hernando de Soto Bridge. It's an ideal location for a peaceful moment in the heart of downtown Memphis.

Memphis is a city of many facets, and its parks and gardens offer a chance to escape the hustle and bustle of the city while enjoying the natural beauty and historical significance of the region. From the expansive Shelby Farms Park to the tranquil beauty of Audubon Park, there are green spaces to suit all interests and preferences. So, during your visit to Memphis, make sure to explore these parks and gardens, each with its unique charm and character, providing a refreshing and memorable experience. Whether you're a history buff, a nature lover, or just seeking a relaxing place to unwind, Memphis has something for everyone in its lush and picturesque outdoor spaces.

Family Friendly attractions and Activities

Memphis, Tennessee host variety of family-friendly attractions and activities that are sure to delight visitors of all ages. Whether you're a history buff, a music lover, or just looking for some good old-fashioned fun, Memphis has something for everyone. we will explore some of the best family-friendly attractions and activities that you can enjoy during your visit to Memphis, complete with addresses to help you plan your trip.

Graceland:
Address: 3717 Elvis Presley Blvd, Memphis, TN 38116
No visit to Memphis would be complete without a trip to Graceland, the former home of the King of Rock 'n' Roll, Elvis Presley. This iconic mansion is a must-see attraction for fans of Elvis and music enthusiasts. Explore the mansion, Elvis's cars, and the Elvis Presley Car Museum. Don't forget to visit Elvis's final resting place in the Meditation Garden.

Memphis Zoo:
Address: 2000 Prentiss Pl, Memphis, TN 38112
The Memphis Zoo is a fantastic place for families to spend a day surrounded by a diverse array of animals from around the world. You can witness giraffes, lions, pandas, and more. The zoo also offers fun educational programs, including animal encounters and live shows.

Stax Museum of American Soul Music:
Address: 926 E McLemore Ave, Memphis, TN 38106
Immerse your family in the history of soul music at the Stax Museum. Explore the origins of soul music and see memorabilia from legendary artists like Otis Redding and Isaac Hayes. It's an educational and entertaining experience that will appeal to music lovers of all ages.

Memphis Botanic Garden:
Address: 750 Cherry Rd, Memphis, TN 38117
For a relaxing day surrounded by the beauty of nature, head to the Memphis Botanic Garden. It features a wide variety of gardens, walking trails, and family-friendly spaces. Kids will love the My Big Backyard area, which offers hands-on educational activities.

Shelby Farms Park:
Address: 6903 Great View Dr N, Memphis, TN 38134
Shelby Farms Park is one of the largest urban parks in the United States, offering countless recreational opportunities. You can bike, hike, have a picnic, or even rent paddle boats at Hyde Lake. The park hosts a variety of family-friendly events throughout the year, so be sure to check their calendar.

Children's Museum of Memphis:
Address: 2525 Central Ave, Memphis, TN 38104
The Children's Museum of Memphis is an interactive wonderland for kids of all ages. It features a wide range of hands-on exhibits, including a model city, a fire engine, and an outdoor play space. Educational and entertaining, this museum is perfect for families.

Mud Island River Park:
Address: 125 N Front St, Memphis, TN 38103
Mud Island River Park is a unique and fun attraction, offering a replica of the Mississippi River and its history. Kids can play in the Riverwalk model, enjoy pedal boats, or attend concerts at the amphitheater. The Mississippi River Museum provides an educational experience.

Memphis Rock 'n' Soul Museum:
Address: 191 Beale St, Memphis, TN 38103

This Smithsonian-affiliated museum delves into the history of rock and soul music in Memphis, where the sounds of legends like Elvis Presley and B.B. King were born. Interactive exhibits make this museum an engaging experience for all ages.

Lichterman Nature Center:
Address: 5992 Quince Rd, Memphis, TN 38119
The Lichterman Nature Center is a 65-acre urban nature preserve, perfect for families interested in wildlife and the environment. You can explore various ecosystems, including woodlands, ponds, and meadows. They often host nature-themed events and educational programs.

Memphis Fire Museum:
Address: 118 Adams Ave, Memphis, TN 38103
The Memphis Fire Museum is an exciting destination for kids and adults alike. Learn about the history of firefighting, explore vintage fire engines, and even slide down a real fire pole. It's an interactive and educational experience.

T.O. Fuller State Park:
Address: 1500 W Mitchell Rd, Memphis, TN 38109
T.O. Fuller State Park is a beautiful outdoor space that offers hiking trails, picnicking areas, and a golf course. It's an excellent place for families to enjoy the great outdoors and have a relaxing day in nature.

National Civil Rights Museum:
Address: 450 Mulberry St, Memphis, TN 38103
The National Civil Rights Museum, located at the site of the Lorraine Motel where Dr. Martin Luther King Jr. was assassinated, is an essential educational experience. It presents the history of the civil rights movement in a way that is accessible to both kids and adults.

Memphis Riverboats:
Address: 45 S Riverside Dr, Memphis, TN 38103
Embark on a river adventure aboard one of the Memphis Riverboats. You can choose from a variety of cruises, including sightseeing tours, dinner cruises, and even pirate-themed adventures. Enjoy stunning views of the Mississippi River while learning about its history.

Dixon Gallery and Gardens:
Address: 4339 Park Ave, Memphis, TN 38117
The Dixon Gallery and Gardens is an art museum set in beautiful gardens. It features a diverse collection of art, including European and American masterpieces. The serene gardens provide a peaceful backdrop for a family visit.

From the music history of Graceland to the interactive exhibits at the Children's Museum of Memphis, there is something for everyone to enjoy. Whether you're exploring the great outdoors at T.O. Fuller State Park or delving into the cultural heritage of the National Civil Rights Museum, Memphis has it all. So, pack your bags, plan your trip, and get ready to create lasting family memories in this vibrant and historic city.

Day Trips and Excursions

Memphis isn't just confined to its city limits. The surrounding areas, within a day's trip, are filled with remarkable destinations that offer a diverse range of experiences. we'll delve into the details of some of the best day trips and excursions you can embark on during your visit to Memphis.

Graceland: The Home of Elvis Presley

Address: 3717 Elvis Presley Blvd, Memphis, TN 38116

Distance from Memphis: 10 miles (approximately a 20-minute drive)

Your journey into the heart of Memphis' cultural heritage begins with a trip to Graceland, the historic home of the King of Rock 'n' Roll, Elvis Presley. This iconic mansion, with its distinct Southern colonial architecture, is not only a significant landmark but also a deeply personal insight into the life of one of music's most legendary figures.

Graceland offers several tours, allowing visitors to explore different facets of this grand estate. The most popular tour takes you through the mansion, giving you a glimpse of Elvis's living quarters, including the famed Jungle Room and the Meditation Garden where Elvis and his family are laid to rest.

Another notable tour option is the Elvis Presley Car Museum, which showcases a collection of his flamboyant cars, including his iconic Pink Cadillac. It's a fascinating way to get up close and personal with the vehicles that accompanied Elvis through his illustrious career.

Overall, Graceland is a must-visit for music aficionados, as it offers a unique opportunity to step back in time and experience the life of a true American music legend.

Shelby Farms Park

Address: 6903 Great View Drive North, Memphis, TN 38134
Distance from Memphis: 13 miles (approximately a 25-minute drive)

Nature lovers and outdoor enthusiasts will find solace in the serene beauty of Shelby Farms Park. As one of the largest urban parks in the United States, it spans over 4,500 acres, providing ample opportunities for recreation, exploration, and relaxation.

The park offers a wide variety of activities, including walking and biking trails, horseback riding, and even paddleboarding on its stunning 80-acre lake. The vast meadows and picnic areas make it an ideal spot for a family outing, a romantic picnic, or a peaceful escape from the city's hustle and bustle.

For those with an adventurous spirit, the park features an extensive zipline course, ensuring an adrenaline rush amidst the serene surroundings. Overall, Shelby Farms Park offers a perfect balance of nature, adventure, and relaxation, making it a day trip you won't forget.

Sun Studio

Address: 706 Union Ave, Memphis, TN 38103
Distance from Memphis: Located in downtown Memphis

Just a stone's throw away from downtown Memphis lies the iconic Sun Studio, often referred to as the "Birthplace of Rock 'n' Roll." This unassuming recording studio holds a special place in the history of music, having witnessed the birth of legendary careers like Elvis Presley, Johnny Cash, and Jerry Lee Lewis.

A guided tour through Sun Studio is a journey back in time to the era when rock 'n' roll was born. You'll stand in the same room where Elvis recorded his first hits and experience the magic that happened within these walls.

The tour also delves into the studio's history, showcasing rare memorabilia and sharing intriguing stories about the artists who shaped the music industry. For any music enthusiast, a visit to Sun Studio is a pilgrimage to the roots of American music.

Mississippi River Park

Address: Riverside Dr, Memphis, TN 38103
Distance from Memphis: Located in downtown Memphis
Strolling along the banks of the mighty Mississippi River is a serene and soul-soothing experience. The Mississippi River Park offers precisely that, with breathtaking views of the river, well-maintained walkways, and an abundance of greenery.

As you amble along, you'll have the chance to appreciate the impressive Hernando de Soto Bridge that spans the river. The park also serves as a fantastic location to have a picnic, play a game of frisbee, or simply relax while taking in the beautiful scenery.

If you're looking for a more immersive experience, consider hopping on a riverboat cruise. These cruises allow you to explore the river from a different perspective, offering narration on the river's history and its significance to Memphis.

T.O. Fuller State Park

Address: 1500 Mitchell Rd, Memphis, TN 38109
Distance from Memphis: 12 miles (approximately a 25-minute drive)

T.O. Fuller State Park is a natural oasis conveniently situated just a short drive from Memphis. This vast park covers over 1,100 acres and provides an array of outdoor activities for visitors.

Hikers and nature enthusiasts can explore the park's various trails, which wind through the lush woodlands and offer glimpses of local wildlife. The golfers among you will appreciate the pristine golf course that's part of the park, complete with scenic views and well-kept greens.

Picnic areas are scattered throughout the park, making it an excellent location for a family outing or a leisurely lunch surrounded by nature. For an all-encompassing experience, take advantage of the on-site campground to extend your stay and immerse yourself in the natural beauty of T.O. Fuller State Park.

National Civil Rights Museum

Address: 450 Mulberry St, Memphis, TN 38103
Distance from Memphis: Located in downtown Memphis

Memphis played a pivotal role in the civil rights movement, and the National Civil Rights Museum stands as a powerful testament to this history. The museum is housed in the former Lorraine Motel, where Dr. Martin Luther King Jr. was tragically assassinated in 1968.

A visit to the National Civil Rights Museum is a deeply moving and educational experience. The museum chronicles the struggles and triumphs of the civil rights movement in the United States. Visitors can explore exhibits that depict the challenges faced by African Americans throughout history, from slavery to the present day.

The centerpiece of the museum is the preserved motel room where Dr. King spent his last hours. Standing in that room is a poignant and emotional experience that leaves a lasting impact on those who visit.

The National Civil Rights Museum serves as a crucial reminder of the ongoing fight for equality and justice, making it an essential destination for anyone interested in the social history of the United States.

Tunica, Mississippi

Address: Tunica, MS 38676
Distance from Memphis: 39 miles (approximately a 45-minute drive)

If you're in the mood for some excitement and entertainment, a trip to Tunica, Mississippi, is just the ticket. Known as the "Casino Capital of the South," Tunica is a hub for gaming and leisure activities.

Numerous casinos line the banks of the Mississippi River, offering a range of games, from slot machines to poker tables. Tunica also boasts world-class dining options and live entertainment venues, ensuring a lively and entertaining day trip.

The Horseshoe Casino and the Gold Strike Casino are two popular destinations, both offering a mix of gaming, dining, and entertainment options. Whether you're trying your luck at the blackjack table or indulging in a sumptuous meal, Tunica provides a blend of excitement and relaxation.

St. Jude Children's Research Hospital

Address: 262 Danny Thomas Place, Memphis, TN 38105
Distance from Memphis: Located in downtown Memphis

While many day trips focus on leisure and recreation, visiting St. Jude Children's Research Hospital offers a meaningful and educational experience. St. Jude is a world-renowned institution dedicated to treating and curing pediatric catastrophic diseases.

While tours inside the hospital itself may not be available due to patient privacy concerns, visitors can explore the beautiful gardens surrounding the facility. The gardens are not only serene and inviting but also provide information about St. Jude's mission and the critical work they do in the field of pediatric medicine.

A visit to St. Jude offers a chance to learn about the hospital's history, its commitment to treating children regardless of their ability to pay, and its groundbreaking research. It's an opportunity to be inspired by the resilience of young patients and the incredible work being done to improve their lives.

Historic Helena, Arkansas

Address: Helena, AR 72342
Distance from Memphis: 75 miles (approximately a 1.5-hour drive)

A short drive across the Mississippi River takes you to the charming town of Helena, Arkansas. This town holds a special place in American history and boasts a rich cultural heritage.

Helena's historic downtown area, anchored by Cherry Street, is filled with beautifully preserved buildings from the late 19th and early 20th centuries. The town's history is deeply intertwined with the Mississippi River, and you can learn about its significance at the Delta Cultural Center.

The center provides a comprehensive view of the region's cultural and historical impact, with exhibits that explore the

Delta's music heritage, the Civil War, and the Mississippi River itself. Visitors can also take a stroll along the Mississippi River levee and take in the scenic views of the river.

Tupelo, Mississippi

Address: Tupelo, MS 38804
Distance from Memphis: 108 miles (approximately a 1.5-hour drive)
Known as the birthplace of Elvis Presley, Tupelo, Mississippi, is a city that pays homage to the legendary musician. A visit to Tupelo allows you to explore the early life and influences of the King of Rock 'n' Roll.

The Elvis Presley Birthplace is a historical site that includes the modest two-room house where Elvis was born in 1935. The home has been restored to its 1930s condition, providing a glimpse into the Presley family's life during that time.

The Birthplace also features a museum with exhibits that detail Elvis's early years, his family, and his rise to fame. A chapel and a park complete the experience, making it a comprehensive and engaging journey into the life of Elvis Presley.

Beyond the Elvis connection, Tupelo offers a charming downtown area with unique shops, restaurants, and a thriving arts scene, making it a delightful destination for a day trip.

Reelfoot Lake State Park

Address: 2595 State Route 21 E, Tiptonville, TN 38079
Distance from Memphis: 132 miles (approximately a 2.5-hour drive)

For those seeking a more extensive natural retreat, Reelfoot Lake State Park is a gem of Northwest Tennessee. The park, centered around a 15,000-acre lake, is a unique and picturesque destination.

The lake itself was created by a series of violent earthquakes in 1811-1812, resulting in sunken forests and submerged cypress trees. The park's diverse ecosystem offers birdwatching enthusiasts a glimpse of a wide variety of avian species, including bald eagles.
Fishing is another popular activity, with the lake being known for its crappie, bluegill, and catfish. Kayaking and canoeing are also excellent ways to explore the lake's distinctive beauty.

The park provides well-maintained trails for hiking and biking, as well as opportunities for picnicking and wildlife photography. Reelfoot Lake State Park is a true natural wonder that allows you to connect with the outdoors and escape into the tranquility of this unique setting.

Memphis Zoo

Address: 2000 Prentiss Pl, Memphis, TN 38112
Distance from Memphis: Located in midtown Memphis

For a family-friendly day trip, the Memphis Zoo is a top-notch choice. This zoo is home to over 3,500 animals, representing more than 500 species from around the world. With its well-designed exhibits and educational programs, it offers an exciting and educational experience for visitors of all ages.

The zoo's well-regarded exhibits include Teton Trek, which replicates the habitats of grizzly bears and wolves, and the

Zambezi River Hippo Camp, featuring an immersive underwater hippo viewing area. The giant panda exhibit is another highlight, as Memphis is one of only a few U.S. zoos to house these beloved animals.

Throughout the year, the Memphis Zoo hosts special events and activities, ensuring that each visit is unique and engaging. The zoo's commitment to conservation and education makes it an excellent destination for families looking to learn more about the animal kingdom.

Each of these day trips and excursions offers a unique experience, allowing you to explore various facets of Memphis and its surroundings. From the music history of Elvis Presley's Graceland to the natural beauty of T.O. Fuller State Park and Reelfoot Lake State Park, there's something for everyone within a short drive from the city. Whether you're interested in history, outdoor adventures, or just a leisurely day out, Memphis and its neighboring destinations provide a wide array of choices for unforgettable experiences. So, pack your bags, plan your itinerary, and embark on a journey of discovery as you explore the wonders that await just beyond Memphis.

Practical Information

Safety and Security Considerations

While Memphis has much to offer, like any other major city, it's essential for visitors to be aware of safety and security considerations to ensure a pleasant and trouble-free trip. we'll delve into the various aspects of staying safe in Memphis, helping you make the most of your visit.

Understanding the City's Neighborhoods:

Memphis is a diverse city with a range of neighborhoods, each offering a unique atmosphere. When planning your visit, it's essential to research these neighborhoods to determine which areas you'll be frequenting and their respective safety levels. Some popular neighborhoods in Memphis include:

Downtown Memphis: Home to Beale Street, the historic district is known for its live music venues, restaurants, and vibrant nightlife. Generally safe for tourists.

Midtown Memphis: A more residential area with a bohemian atmosphere, it's known for its historic homes and cultural attractions. It's also considered safe for visitors.

East Memphis: A commercial and business district, it's relatively safe with upscale dining and shopping options.

South Memphis: Some parts of South Memphis may have higher crime rates, so it's best to be cautious when visiting this area.

Avoiding High Crime Areas:

While Memphis has much to offer, it's not without its challenges. Some areas of the city have higher crime rates than others, and it's advisable for visitors to steer clear of these regions. Places like Frayser and North Memphis have higher crime rates, and it's best to exercise caution if you find yourself in these areas.

Personal Safety Tips:
To ensure your safety while exploring Memphis, consider the following tips:

Travel in groups: Whenever possible, explore the city with a group of friends or fellow travelers. There is safety in numbers, and it's less likely for potential threats to approach a group.

Keep your belongings secure: Like in any other city, be mindful of your personal belongings. Use crossbody bags, money belts, or anti-theft backpacks to deter pickpockets.

Be aware of your surroundings: Stay vigilant and avoid distractions, especially when using your phone. Knowing what's happening around you can help you react to potential dangers.

Stick to well-lit areas: When walking around the city at night, choose well-lit streets and avoid dimly lit alleys or areas with limited visibility.

Transportation Safety:
Getting around Memphis can be relatively safe if you follow these tips:

Use reputable transportation services: Stick to recognized taxi services, rideshare apps, or public transportation options. Verify the identity of your driver before getting into a vehicle.

Park in well-lit areas: If you have a rental car, make sure to park it in well-lit and safe areas. Avoid leaving valuables in plain sight.

Be cautious on public transport: While Memphis has a bus system, exercise caution when using it, especially at night. Keep an eye on your belongings.

Homelessness and Panhandling:
Memphis, like many other cities, has a visible homeless population, particularly in certain downtown areas. While most of the homeless individuals are harmless, it's best to handle panhandling situations with care. If you choose to give, do so discreetly, and avoid engaging in lengthy conversations that might make you uncomfortable.

Emergency Contact Information:
Prior to your visit, ensure you have a list of emergency contact information. This should include:

Memphis Police Department: 911 (for emergencies) or 901-545-COPS (non-emergency).

Local hospitals and medical facilities: In case of accidents or health emergencies, have a list of nearby medical facilities and their contact information.

U.S. Embassy or Consulate: If you're an international visitor, know the location and contact information for your nearest embassy or consulate.

Cultural Sensitivity:
Memphis is known for its rich cultural heritage, and visitors should be respectful and sensitive to the local customs and traditions. While Memphis is generally a welcoming city, it's

always a good practice to be courteous and considerate of the local culture.

While there are safety and security considerations to keep in mind during your visit, with some awareness and preparation, you can have a memorable and safe experience in this iconic city. Remember to do your research, stay aware of your surroundings, and follow the local advice to make the most of your trip while staying safe. Enjoy the music, food, and hospitality that Memphis has to offer, and you'll leave with fond memories of this unique Southern gem.

Transportation & Getting around

When you visit Memphis, you'll want to explore everything this city has to offer, from Graceland to Beale Street. To make the most of your trip, it's essential to have a solid understanding of transportation options and how to get around efficiently. In this comprehensive guide, we'll explore various transportation methods available in Memphis, including public transportation, rental cars, rideshares, and even walking and biking.

Public Transportation

Memphis Area Transit Authority (MATA)

The Memphis Area Transit Authority (MATA) is the primary provider of public transportation in Memphis. MATA operates a network of buses and trolley services that can help you navigate the city efficiently. Here are some key details about MATA:

Bus Routes:
MATA (Memphis Area Transit Authority) plays a pivotal role in providing efficient and accessible public transportation throughout Memphis. The bus network is a lifeline for locals

and visitors alike, connecting various neighborhoods, must-visit attractions, and the bustling downtown area. With its wide-reaching routes, MATA offers an affordable and convenient way to explore Memphis.

MATA's extensive network of bus routes covers the entire city, ensuring you can reach your desired destinations without much hassle. Here are some key features of the bus system:

Neighborhood Accessibility: MATA buses reach every nook and cranny of Memphis, allowing you to dive into the heart of different neighborhoods and experience the city's diverse culture. From the historic architecture of Victorian Village to the lively energy of Midtown, you can easily access Memphis' unique districts.

Tourist Attractions: MATA has strategically designed its routes to make sure you can access the city's iconic tourist attractions. Whether you're eager to explore the profound history of the National Civil Rights Museum, savor the music and nightlife on Beale Street, or soak in the scenic beauty of the Mississippi Riverfront, MATA buses can get you there.

Affordable Options: MATA offers flexible fare options, allowing you to choose the one that best suits your needs. You can purchase single-ride tickets or opt for day passes, which are perfect for tourists looking to make multiple stops in a single day. For those planning an extended stay in Memphis, monthly passes provide further cost-effective alternatives.

Trolley Services:
One of Memphis's unique transportation offerings is the Main Street Trolley, which adds a delightful, historic twist to your exploration of the city. The trolley service runs through

downtown Memphis and is a must-try for those who wish to immerse themselves in the city's rich heritage and culture. Here's why the Main Street Trolley is a standout option:

Historic Charm: The Main Street Trolley is not just a mode of transportation; it's an experience. These vintage trolleys harken back to a bygone era, and the charming, old-world ambiance is sure to transport you to a different time. As you glide through the streets, you'll appreciate the unique character and charm of Memphis.

Central Attractions: The trolley route conveniently covers many of the city's central attractions. It's the perfect choice for tourists who want to hop on and off while exploring landmarks such as the National Civil Rights Museum, where the civil rights movement's history is brought to life, or the lively and legendary Beale Street, known for its music and entertainment.

Riverfront Experience: The trolley offers a picturesque route along the Mississippi Riverfront. This scenic journey is an opportunity to enjoy stunning river views and take in the serenity of the flowing waters.

Fares and Passes:
To make your experience with MATA seamless and cost-effective, you'll want to explore the fare options available. MATA understands that visitors have varying needs, and they offer a range of fare choices to accommodate your stay in Memphis:

Single-Ride Tickets: If you're planning just a few bus rides or trolley journeys during your visit, single-ride tickets are a convenient choice. They allow you to pay for each ride individually.

Day Passes: Day passes are ideal for travelers who intend to explore the city extensively in a single day. These passes provide unlimited access to MATA services for a 24-hour period, offering excellent value for money.

Monthly Passes: For those staying in Memphis for an extended period or who anticipate frequent use of public transportation, monthly passes offer the best long-term value. They grant unlimited access to MATA buses and trolleys for an entire month.

MATA's fare information, including pricing and any updates, can be found on their website. It's advisable to check their website or contact their customer service for the most up-to-date fare details and any special promotions that might be available during your visit.

Rental Cars

If you prefer the flexibility and convenience of having your own vehicle during your stay in Memphis, renting a car is a viable option. There are several rental car companies operating at Memphis International Airport, as well as various locations throughout the city. Here's what you need to know about renting a car in Memphis:

Rental Agencies: Popular rental car agencies, such as Enterprise, Hertz, Avis, and Budget, have counters at Memphis International Airport. It's advisable to book your car rental in advance to secure the best rates and availability.

Parking: Memphis offers a range of parking options, including street parking, parking garages, and parking lots. Be sure to check parking rates and time limits, as they may vary from one location to another.

Traffic and Navigation: Memphis has a well-connected road system. However, like any major city, you may encounter traffic congestion, especially during peak hours. Make use of GPS or navigation apps to help you navigate the city efficiently.

Ridesharing Services

Ridesharing services like Uber and Lyft are readily available in Memphis. These platforms offer a convenient way to get around the city without the hassle of driving or parking. Here are some key points to consider when using ridesharing services:

Accessibility: Uber and Lyft drivers are generally easy to find throughout Memphis, making it a reliable way to get from one place to another, whether you're heading to a tourist attraction or a local eatery.

Cost: The cost of ridesharing services can vary depending on factors like distance, time of day, and demand. These services are often more expensive than public transportation but can be more affordable than renting a car.

Ride Scheduling: You can schedule rides in advance, which is particularly useful for early morning flights or important appointments.

Biking

Memphis has taken steps to become more bike-friendly in recent years, making cycling a viable option for exploring the city. Here's what you need to know about biking in Memphis:

Bike Lanes and Paths: Memphis has a growing network of bike lanes and paths, including the Mississippi River

Greenbelt Park and the Shelby Farms Greenline. These dedicated routes make it safer and more enjoyable to bike around the city.

Bike Rentals: If you didn't bring your own bike, don't worry. There are bike rental shops and services in Memphis that offer both traditional bicycles and electric bikes.

Biking Tours: Consider taking a guided biking tour to explore Memphis while learning about its history and culture. These tours often include stops at famous landmarks and eateries.

Walking

Exploring Memphis on foot is an excellent way to soak in the city's unique atmosphere and discover hidden gems. Many of the city's attractions, restaurants, and shops are within walking distance of each other, especially in downtown Memphis. Here are some tips for walking around the city:

Comfortable Footwear: Wear comfortable walking shoes to ensure you can explore Memphis on foot without discomfort. The city's sidewalks and streets are generally pedestrian-friendly.

Historic Walking Tours: Memphis offers a range of guided walking tours that provide insights into its history, music scene, and civil rights movement. Walking tours are a great way to learn more about the city while staying active.

Safety: Like any urban environment, it's essential to remain aware of your surroundings while walking. Stick to well-lit areas, and take the necessary precautions to keep your belongings secure.

Memphis is a city that offers a wide array of transportation options to suit the preferences of every visitor. Whether you choose to explore the city using public transportation, rent a car, utilize ridesharing services, bike, or simply walk, Memphis is a destination that is accessible and accommodating to all travelers. By understanding the various transportation methods available, you can make the most of your visit and experience everything this vibrant city has to offer, from the legendary Beale Street to the hallowed grounds of Graceland, with ease and convenience.

Money Matters and Currency Exchange

One of these crucial factors is managing your finances and understanding currency exchange. Whether you're a domestic traveler or visiting from abroad, having a good grasp of money matters can make your experience in the "Home of the Blues" and the "Birthplace of Rock 'n' Roll" even more enjoyable.

Understanding the US Dollar

Memphis, like the rest of the United States, uses the US dollar (USD) as its official currency. The US dollar is denominated in coins (cents) and banknotes (bills) with various denominations, including $1, $5, $10, $20, $50, and $100. It's essential to familiarize yourself with these denominations to make transactions more manageable.

Currency Exchange

If you're traveling from another country, you'll likely need to exchange your home currency for US dollars. Here's what you need to know about currency exchange in Memphis:

Airport Exchanges: Upon arriving at Memphis International Airport, you'll find currency exchange counters where you can exchange your money. While convenient, these services often offer less favorable exchange rates and may charge higher fees. It's advisable to exchange only a small amount at the airport and wait until you're in the city for better rates.

Local Banks: Banks are a reliable place to exchange currency, and you'll often receive more favorable rates than at the airport. However, banks may charge service fees for currency exchange, so be sure to inquire about these fees before proceeding with the exchange.

ATMs: Using ATMs is a convenient way to obtain US dollars. Memphis has an extensive network of ATMs that accept international cards, but be aware of any foreign transaction fees that your bank may charge. Additionally, check with your bank to ensure your card will work in the United States.

Currency Exchange Offices: In Memphis, you can find dedicated currency exchange offices that often offer competitive rates and low fees compared to airports and hotels. Before using such services, it's a good idea to check online or call ahead to compare rates.

Credit and Debit Cards: Most businesses in Memphis, including hotels, restaurants, and retail shops, accept major credit and debit cards, making it easy to pay without having to carry a lot of cash. However, it's a good idea to inform your bank about your travel plans to avoid any issues with your cards.

Tips for Handling Cash

While electronic payments are widely accepted, you'll still need cash for some situations, such as small purchases, tipping, or places that may not accept cards. Here are some tips for handling cash during your visit to Memphis:

Tipping: In the United States, tipping is customary in various service industries. A typical guideline is to tip 15-20% of the total bill in restaurants. For other services like taxis, hotels, and tour guides, tipping is also expected.

Safety: Memphis, like any other city, has its share of petty crime. Be cautious when carrying cash and avoid displaying large sums in public. It's a good idea to use a money belt or a concealed pouch to store your cash and important documents.

ATMs: Use ATMs located in well-lit, secure areas, and be aware of your surroundings when withdrawing cash. If you need to withdraw cash at night, choose ATMs located inside banks or secure facilities.

Check for Fees: Keep an eye out for fees associated with using ATMs, exchanging currency, or making card transactions. These fees can add up, so it's essential to plan your finances accordingly.

Budgeting for Your Trip

Memphis offers a wide range of attractions and activities, and how much you'll spend during your visit depends on your preferences and travel style. However, here's a rough estimate of some common expenses to help you plan your budget:

Accommodation: Memphis offers a variety of lodging options, from budget-friendly motels to upscale hotels. Prices can vary greatly, with budget options starting at around $50 per night and higher-end hotels costing $150 or more per night.

Food: Dining in Memphis is a highlight of the trip, especially if you're a fan of barbecue. On average, you can expect to spend $10-20 for a meal at a casual restaurant, and more for upscale dining experiences.

Transportation: If you're using public transportation, like buses, you can expect to pay around $1.75 for a one-way ticket. Taxis and ride-sharing services are also available.

Attractions: Memphis is known for its rich music history, and visiting attractions like Graceland or the Stax Museum can cost around $20-30 per person. Some attractions offer combo tickets to help you save on admission fees.

Entertainment: Memphis has a vibrant nightlife, with live music venues, bars, and clubs. Plan to spend $10-20 on cover charges or tickets for live performances, plus the cost of drinks.

Shopping: Be sure to allocate a budget for shopping, whether it's for souvenirs, clothing, or antiques. Prices can vary widely, but it's easy to find unique items to take home as a memory of your trip.

Currency Exchange Tips for International Travelers

If you're visiting Memphis from another country, consider these additional currency exchange tips:

Exchange Some Currency in Advance: It's a good idea to exchange a small amount of US dollars in your home country before you travel. This way, you'll have cash on hand for immediate expenses upon arrival.

Use a Currency Conversion App: There are several smartphone apps that can help you convert prices into your home currency, making it easier to budget and compare costs.

Notify Your Bank: Let your bank know about your travel plans to Memphis to avoid having your card blocked due to suspicious activity. It's also advisable to carry a backup card or source of funds.

Keep Records: Whenever you exchange currency or make financial transactions, keep records of the rates and fees you're charged. This can be helpful for tracking your expenses and potentially filing for refunds if necessary.

With careful planning, budgeting, and an understanding of currency exchange options, you can make the most of your time in the vibrant city, exploring its rich music history, savoring delicious food, and taking in the unique cultural experiences that Memphis has to offer. By being well-prepared, you can make your visit to the "Home of the Blues" and the "Birthplace of Rock 'n' Roll" a memorable and financially sound adventure.

Health Precautions

When planning a visit to Memphis, it's essential to ensure you take necessary health precautions to have a safe and enjoyable trip. we'll discuss various health precautions to keep in mind while exploring this incredible city, from staying hydrated in the humid weather to being cautious about local cuisine and understanding potential health risks.

Weather Precautions:

Memphis experiences a humid subtropical climate, with hot and humid summers and mild winters. While this climate can be enjoyable, it's crucial to take precautions to protect your health. Here are some tips to consider:

- Stay hydrated: The high temperatures and humidity can lead to dehydration. Always carry a refillable water bottle and drink plenty of water throughout the day.
- Sun protection: Memphis can get scorching during the summer, so apply sunscreen and wear sunglasses and a wide-brimmed hat to protect your skin and eyes from the sun's harmful rays.
- Dress appropriately: Wear lightweight, breathable clothing to stay comfortable in the heat, and consider packing an umbrella or a light rain jacket in case of sudden rain showers.

Food Safety:

Memphis is famous for its delectable barbecue and soul food. While indulging in these mouthwatering dishes is a must, it's crucial to be mindful of food safety to prevent foodborne illnesses. Here are some tips:

- Choose reputable restaurants: Opt for well-established eateries with good hygiene practices. Read reviews and ask locals for recommendations.
- Wash your hands: Before eating, make sure to wash your hands thoroughly with soap and water, or use hand sanitizer.
- Avoid tap water: It's generally recommended to drink bottled or filtered water to prevent any stomach discomfort.

Allergies:

If you have food allergies, be sure to communicate your dietary restrictions clearly when dining out in Memphis. Most restaurants are accommodating and can provide allergen-free options. Carry any necessary medications or allergy cards in case of an emergency.

Hydration:

With the high temperatures and humidity, it's easy to become dehydrated while exploring Memphis. Carry a reusable water bottle and refill it regularly. Drinking plenty of water not only keeps you refreshed but also helps ward off heat-related illnesses.

Insect Precautions:

Memphis, like many Southern cities, has its share of mosquitoes and other insects, especially during the warmer months. Protect yourself from insect bites to prevent diseases such as West Nile virus. Here's what you can do:

- Use insect repellent: Apply insect repellent with DEET to exposed skin and clothing to deter mosquitoes and other insects.
- Wear protective clothing: Long-sleeved shirts and pants can help reduce your exposure to insect bites.
- Stay indoors during peak mosquito activity: Mosquitoes are most active during dawn and dusk, so plan your outdoor activities accordingly.

Stay Active and Fit:

While exploring Memphis, take advantage of the city's numerous parks and recreational opportunities. Walking along the Mississippi River, visiting Shelby Farms Park, or taking a stroll down Beale Street can be great ways to stay active. Regular exercise not only helps you stay fit but also boosts your immune system.

First Aid Kit:

Carrying a small first aid kit can be a lifesaver. Include items like adhesive bandages, pain relievers, antacids, and any specific medications you may need. It's always better to be prepared for minor health issues.

Stay Informed:

Before and during your trip, keep yourself updated on the latest health advisories and local news. Being aware of any local health concerns or emergencies can help you make informed decisions.

Emergency Services:

Familiarize yourself with the local emergency numbers, such as 911, and the nearest healthcare facilities. It's always a good idea to know where to seek medical assistance if needed.

By taking these health precautions into account, you can ensure a memorable and worry-free experience in this vibrant city. Remember to stay hydrated, protect yourself from the elements, be mindful of food safety, and stay informed about any potential health risks during your visit. Enjoy your time in Memphis and make lasting memories while staying healthy.

Emergency contact numbers

While Memphis is a vibrant and exciting city with a rich cultural heritage and plenty of attractions to explore, like Graceland, Beale Street, and the National Civil Rights Museum, it's always prudent to have a list of emergency contact numbers readily available. We will provide you with essential emergency numbers to ensure a smooth and safe visit to Memphis.

1. 911 - Emergency Services

In the United States, 911 is the universal emergency number for police, fire, and medical emergencies. It should be the first number you dial if you find yourself in any dire situation. The dispatcher will connect you to the appropriate emergency service.

2. Memphis Police Department

Memphis has its own police department, which is responsible for maintaining law and order within the city. If you encounter a non-emergency situation or require assistance from the police that doesn't require an immediate response, you can contact the Memphis Police Department at (901) 545-2677. This number is suitable for reporting incidents such as theft, lost property, or filing a police report.

3. Memphis Fire Department

In case of a fire emergency, dial 911 immediately. However, for non-emergency inquiries related to fire safety or to report a fire hazard, you can contact the Memphis Fire Department at (901) 636-1400.

4. Medical Emergencies

For medical emergencies, Memphis is home to several hospitals and medical facilities. The following are some of the major hospitals in Memphis where you can seek medical assistance:

Methodist University Hospital: Located in the Medical District, Methodist University Hospital is known for its excellent medical care. In case of a medical emergency, call (901) 516-7000.

St. Jude Children's Research Hospital: If your child needs immediate medical attention, St. Jude Children's Research Hospital is a world-renowned institution. Call (901) 595-3300 for assistance.

Regional One Health: This Level 1 Trauma Center and teaching hospital provides comprehensive healthcare services. In case of a medical emergency, call (901) 545-7100.

Le Bonheur Children's Hospital: For pediatric emergencies, Le Bonheur Children's Hospital is a top choice. Dial (901) 287-5437 for assistance.

5. Poison Control Center

In the event of a poisoning emergency, contact the Tennessee Poison Control Center at 1-800-222-1222. The experts at the poison control center can provide immediate guidance to manage the situation and prevent further harm.

6. Animal Control

If you encounter a stray or aggressive animal, or if you need assistance with animal-related emergencies, you can contact Memphis Animal Services at (901) 636-1438.

7. Non-Emergency Services

For non-emergency situations that require city services, such as reporting a pothole, utility issues, or city-related inquiries, you can dial 311 or (901) 636-6500. The 311 service is designed to help residents and visitors connect with the appropriate city department for assistance.

8. Emergency Roadside Assistance

If you experience car trouble during your visit to Memphis, you can contact emergency roadside assistance services such as AAA (American Automobile Association) at 1-800-222-4357 or a reputable local towing service.

9. Embassy and Consulate Contacts

For international visitors, it's a good idea to have your country's embassy or consulate contact information handy in case you encounter any issues related to your nationality. These offices can provide assistance with passport issues, legal matters, and other consular services. You can usually find this information on your country's government website or through the local consulate directory.

10. Memphis Tourism Information

In the case of minor emergencies, such as getting lost, needing assistance with directions, or looking for recommendations, you can contact the Memphis Convention & Visitors Bureau at (901) 543-5300. They can provide you with information, maps, and guidance to ensure a smooth stay in the city.

11. Hotel Front Desk

If you're staying at a hotel in Memphis, the front desk is often a helpful resource for various situations, including medical emergencies, lost belongings, or general inquiries. Make sure to have your hotel's contact information readily available.

12. Personal Emergency Contacts

Don't forget to have your own emergency contacts on hand, such as family members, friends, or travel companions. Ensure they have a way to reach you in case of an emergency and that you have a way to contact them as well.

While Memphis is generally a safe and welcoming city for visitors, it's always wise to be prepared for any unforeseen circumstances. Having these emergency contact numbers readily available can help ensure your visit to Memphis is not only enjoyable but also safe and secure.

Safety Tips for Visitors to Memphis

In addition to having access to emergency contact numbers, here are some safety tips to keep in mind when visiting Memphis:

- Stay Aware: Be aware of your surroundings at all times, especially in crowded or unfamiliar areas. Avoid walking alone late at night, and be cautious when using headphones or looking at your phone.

- Lock Your Vehicle: If you're traveling by car, always lock your vehicle and avoid leaving valuables in plain sight. Auto break-ins can happen, so take precautions.

- Keep Valuables Secure: Be mindful of your belongings, such as wallets, purses, and electronic devices. It's advisable to carry only what you need for the day and use a money belt or secure bag for important items.

- Use Reputable Transportation Services: When using ride-sharing services or taxis, ensure that the vehicle and driver match the description provided by the service.

- Stay In Well-Lit Areas: Stick to well-lit streets and avoid dark, isolated areas, especially at night. It's best to walk in groups or pairs.

- Trust Your Instincts: If something doesn't feel right or you sense danger, trust your instincts and take appropriate action, such as moving to a public place or contacting law enforcement.

- Be Mindful of Traffic: Always use crosswalks and obey traffic rules when walking or driving. Memphis, like any city, has its share of traffic, so exercise caution.

- Respect Local Laws: Familiarize yourself with local laws and regulations, and be respectful of the city's cultural and historical sites.

By following these safety tips and keeping emergency contact numbers on hand, you can make the most of your visit to Memphis while ensuring a safe and memorable experience. Enjoy the music, history, and vibrant culture that this iconic city has to offer!

Conclusion

In conclusion, the "Memphis Travel Guide" is not just a book; it's your key to unlocking the vibrant and soulful heart of this incredible city. As we come to the end of this journey through the birthplace of the blues and the home of some of the world's most renowned music, we are left with a deep appreciation for the rich history, culture, and diversity that make Memphis a unique and unforgettable destination.

This guide has strived to provide you with a comprehensive view of Memphis, whether you are a first-time visitor or a returning traveler seeking new experiences. From the iconic Beale Street and Sun Studio to the lesser-known gems like the Memphis Zoo or the Shelby Farms Greenline, this book has offered a detailed exploration of the city's attractions. We've helped you navigate the dynamic culinary scene, ensuring you've tasted the best barbeque in the world and sipped on sweet, authentic soul food. And we've guided you through the historic landmarks, helping you connect with the roots of American music, civil rights, and cultural heritage.

Memphis is not just a destination; it's an experience. The local hospitality, the warm smiles you'll encounter on every corner, and the genuine friendliness of Memphians make your trip here more than just a vacation—it's a connection with the heart and soul of a city that's brimming with character and charisma.

Moreover, Memphis has continuously evolved, offering something for everyone. You can dive deep into its rich past, but also witness its promising future through the revitalization of neighborhoods like Crosstown and South Main. The ever-expanding culinary scene showcases Memphis's appetite for creativity and innovation. Whether you are indulging in classic Southern comfort food or embracing trendy farm-to-table cuisine, there's always a sense of adventure in every bite.

Our journey through Memphis wouldn't be complete without mentioning the significance of music in this city. Memphis is not just a place where music was created; it's a place where music lives and breathes. Be it a visit to the Stax Museum or catching an impromptu jam session on Beale Street, the city offers you a unique chance to experience the raw, emotional power of music that has touched hearts across the globe. We've guided you to explore not only the legends of the past but also the emerging talents that are carrying the legacy forward.

The diverse and eclectic blend of cultures in Memphis is something to be celebrated. You've had a taste of soul, blues, gospel, and rock 'n' roll, and you've seen how these genres have merged and cross-pollinated to create something truly extraordinary. Memphis is a melting pot of cultures, and that is reflected in the art, food, and festivals that make this city so alive.

As you prepare to depart from Memphis, remember that this journey does not end with the closing of this guidebook. Memphis will stay with you, its echoes of music and history lingering in your heart. The friendships you've made, the stories you've heard, and the flavors you've savored will stay with you long after you've left.

In the grand finale of your Memphis experience, this guide hopes to have ignited your passion for exploration, fostered a sense of wonder for the city, and provided you with the tools to create lasting memories. Whether you were here for the music, the food, the history, or simply to soak in the vibrant atmosphere, Memphis has left an indelible mark on your traveler's soul.

In closing, we urge you to come back to Memphis whenever you can. For there is always something new to discover, another rhythm to feel, and another bite of delicious soul food to savor. This city is an ever-evolving masterpiece, a canvas that is painted anew with each sunrise. So, embrace the river, the rhythm, and the remarkable spirit of Memphis. The "Memphis Travel Guide" has been your companion in this extraordinary journey, but your adventure is far from over. Memphis is waiting for you to uncover more of its captivating stories, and we are confident you will return to create new memories in this city that truly never stops singing.

Made in the USA
Monee, IL
23 April 2024

57397747R00105